S0-EPS-750

SEASONS OF THE SPIRIT

by
Hilarion

Copyright © 1980 by
Marcus Books, 195 Randolph Rd.,
Toronto, Canada, M4G 3S6

First printing: October, 1979
Second printing: March, 1980

All rights reserved.

No part of this book may be reproduced in any
form without the permission of the publishers.

Printed and bound in Canada
Cover by Susan Wintrop.

Introduction to the Second Printing

Many readers of this book will already be familiar with the first in this series of books, called *The Nature of Reality*. Both works were 'dictated' to me from a non-physical source who gives his name as Hilarion, through a process in which my conscious mind is stilled deliberately so that a form of telepathy can take place. The procedure involves a technique known in mental or 'Raja' yoga, and is familiar to many who have studied the eastern philosophies. The material I receive in this way is simply copied down directly.

This entire book was transmitted without any apparent division into subject or chapter heads. Indeed, the shifting from one topic to another is in many cases so subtle that one does not even become aware that the focus has changed. Rather than artificially chop the text into awkward fragments, it was decided to print it as given.

The areas with which this book deals are varied. The Great Pyramid, the symbolic meaning of the sea, the Flood, Tiahuanaco—these topics form part of the broad historical panorama which Hilarion discusses. In addition, there is an in-depth treatment of many symbolic areas of significance, including the nose, the eyes, the hand, the leg and the fingernails. He describes the seven main chakras or energy centers of the aetheric body; he details the between-life experiences of each soul; and he treats the subject of astrology from a more spiritual viewpoint than is normally adopted on the earth. A translation of the Gate of the Sun at Tiahuanaco is included in the text, and this forms the basis for the beautiful calligraphic medallion which Toronto artist Susan Wintrop prepared especially for the cover of this book.

In the powerful closing pages of this text, a direct message to the reader is given—one which will remain with him long after he has laid the book aside.

I believe that each soul knows the truth about man and about itself at the core of its being. In publishing this material I hope only that it will allow many to discover a deeper access to their own truths, and to come more into touch with their own inner realities. Unless we as a race can find a new spiritual perspective from which to view ourselves, I fear that we shall never learn to live in peace, to rise above the illusions of selfishness and hatred, or to take our rightful place in the Cosmos.

Maurice B. Cooke
Toronto, Canada.
January, 1980

SEASONS OF THE SPIRIT

Sons and daughters of the Light, believe in yourselves, & believing, reach out to the children whom you have come to teach & uplift. Choose your words always within the compass of their understanding.

The Earth is the home of a race destined for greatness within the cosmos. Do not think of them as slow or backward, for they have come from the God of All that is, as you have, and their destiny is to return, as is yours. They sail upon the seas of this planet as you have traversed the aethers of space. Their bravery and courage are a match for your own. As to the budding Greek civilisation, remember that they hunger in the soul for the gifts of writing, language and history. In them especially the written word lies folded as a flower, waiting to open in splendor. Seek to foster that unfoldment to its fullest bloom, for their language is to be a mighty voice across the ages to come, and the history they write will ripen the race to its maturity.

HILARION

Seasons of the Spirit

The history which man can read in his written records is but part of the great saga which the race has engraved upon the aethers of space. The part which lies hidden behind the veils of time is far greater and far more astounding than anything which appears in the chronicles that remain today. The purpose of this treatise is to set forth the main stages in the development of man as a race within the Cosmos, and to show why it is at last time to lay the full weight of his past upon his conscious mind.

"In the beginning..." So starts the most ancient of man's holy writings concerning the origin of his species. Yet the book of Genesis in the Judeo-Christian Bible is but a partial recounting of the real events that lie at the beginning of man's time. Much has been deliberately distorted in that book, and though the changes were essential in order to hide certain parts of the truth from man's eyes during the aeons of disbelief, still those who were responsible for altering the words of God have had to pay the price which the great Law of Karma exacts for interference with direct revelation. This price is heavy, for it is the loss of all true revelatory contact and inspiration for those who were responsible.

We will start at the beginning in terms of the cycles of time which involve this planet. We do not imply that man has no history prior to his advent upon this earth, for man has always existed and will always exist. But the concept of the everlasting nature of man cannot be grasped by the conscious mind whose patterns of thought are still tied to the passage of time. The illusions of past, present and future must remain with man until his own mind is capable of transcending the barriers that separate his thought patterns from those available on the higher planes of reality.

The first breathing of the human race upon this planet was many millions of years ago as time is measured, and yet it seems to the soul but a short space. In reality the distance of past events in time is a complete illusion and has no meaning as seen from higher planes. For the simple fact is that all of man's past actions remain ever with him, as part of a composite picture or pattern which cannot be altered in any way. The parts of the pattern arising in lives lived a million years ago are just as real and have just as pronounced an influence on the present as those which arise from the present life, or one lived in the last century. Since the present existence of these "past" parts is their only meaningful characteristic, it is clearly of no concern just when they originally arose.

The difficult concept just presented—that all of the past is in a real sense present now—is one expression of the great Law of Karma which governs all realms of Creation from the very highest and most spiritual down to the very lowest and furthest from the central Light. This law has its effect in every aspect of man's existence and at every level of thought, emotion and deed. It is among the purposes of this work to lay before man's understanding a deeper grasp of this great Cosmic Law than has hitherto been available, for in the new age about to burst in glory upon this planet, it will be necessary for man to understand fully the implications of the Karmic Law in order for him to advance as quickly as is intended into the higher realms of achievement and evolution.

In the eastern cultures, the Law of Karma has been misinterpreted in many ways. The true understanding was revealed to the ancient sages by direct revelation many millions of years ago, and the hope was that these advanced souls would be able to preserve for their brothers a clear picture of the meaning and operation of Karma as it affected man's life in the earth. But those who followed after the great sages were not equal to the burden that they had inherited, and certain essential principles were lost.

Among the greatest distortions of the notion of Karma is that which was and still is found among the Hindus of India, particularly those who have not given any time or effort to the study or contemplation of the magnificent religious structure into which they were born. Too often the Karmic principle has been used as an excuse not to reach out and help those who suffered poverty, illness or deformity, on the grounds that to do so would be to "interfere" with the Karma of that afflicted soul. An erroneous belief sprang up that such interference would attract the Karma of the sufferer to the person attempting to help, and this notion was seized upon by the mean and selfish souls who did not want to feel obliged to give of themselves to their brothers. Of course, the truth is the very reverse of this heartless notion, for the refusal to help another who is in need will *by itself* create a Karmic burden for him who refuses.

Yet another misconception is also found in the eastern cultures, even among the religious men and others who profess to have studied the ancient teachings. This is the mistaken idea that Karma somehow involves the concept of *punishment*. Nothing could be further from the truth. Not only is the working out of Karma not a punishment, but it is actually one of the greatest gifts that the Creator of All that Is has made to His children. For without the Karmic Law, none of the myriads of creatures who have emanated from the Mother-Father-God *could ever have begun to find their way back to Him.* All of the divine sparks at the soul-centers of the created beings would eventually have been extinguished and the "evolution of return" toward the Creator's light could never have been initiated.

But a further point remains to be elucidated. Karma has nothing to do with punishment, as we have said. No self-appointed judge sits upon a high throne to pass sentence upon the poor souls who have defied the Laws of Creation and brought pain to others. The Lords of Karma—often thought of as dispensing sentences of Karmic punishment—have a completely different function from that which most people imagine upon hearing their title.

The most important fact to underline in regard to Karma is its *automatic* nature. No entity, not even God Himself, needs to decide whether or not a particular act "deserves" to have some Karma attached to it. For it is a part of the natural functioning of the created worlds that every act in time remains ever with the soul or being who performed the act, as if the action were frozen or stuck to that being. If the nature of the adhering past actions is primarily that of pain or torment caused to other creatures, then the load upon one's shoulders is heavy, dark and hindering in terms of soul-advancement. If the adhering Karma arises mainly from beneficial actions motivated by love or kindness, then the "load" is really not a load at all, but rather a beautiful halo of light and love whose buoyancy in spiritual terms acts like a lighter-than-air baloon which lifts the soul ever higher toward the source of all light.

Karma means simply "action", and it can be seen from the foregoing discussion that the present reality of all past action is at the heart of a correct grasp of the Karmic Principle.

We have explained the main point about Karma, namely that it is an automatic accumulation of all past action around the being or entity responsible for that action. However, the matter is more complex than this, for if there were no means of ridding oneself of the negative or dark Karma arising from actions which bring pain or suffering to others, then no amount of positive or loving action could fully offset that negativity and the soul would not be able to progress higher. Think again of the analogy of the lighter-than-air balloon. Imagine that the soul is a passenger in the basket supported by the balloon. Every negative action of the soul adds lead weights to the basket and tends to drag the balloon and its passenger lower, while every positive, loving or nurturing action toward others fills the balloon with extra gas of the kind which produces lift. The soul is on a journey up away from the earth level, and seeks to rise up through the atmosphere toward the light of spirituality above. But as long as there is any lead weight in the basket, the upward progress is limited and can proceed only to a certain point—this in spite of the fact that the soul can add additional buoyancy to the balloon by positive actions. It is as if there were a barrier which admits no lead weight through, beyond which the soul cannot progress until virtually all of the negative Karma (lead weight) is somehow dropped away from the basket, so that upward progress will no longer be hindered.

The Great God of All That Is has allowed a procedure by

which the negative Karma can be got rid of, to free the balloon for further upward flight. This procedure involves a kind of "discharge" of the negative Karmic burden through the being or body of the entity who has accumulated it. Think of the matter in electrical terms. The build-up of negative Karma through actions causing pain to others can be compared to the charging of storage batteries which are carried about by the soul responsible for the actions. The more negative actions, the greater the electrical charge. Until the electrical energy of the batteries can be discharged, the batteries themselves cannot be discarded, and will remain to impede the spiritual progress of the soul.

With only minor exceptions, the sole manner of discharging these batteries is to take the electrical energy directly through oneself, i.e. to short-circuit the batteries through one's own body. In reality this symbolic discharge is accomplished by passing through experiences of pain and suffering which are the same as or equivalent to the pain and suffering which was caused to others and which resulted in the accumulation of the negative Karma. In every such experience of suffering by any human being, negative Karma is being set aside. No experience of pain is left "unused" in Karmic terms, for there is such a great burden of Karmic negativity upon the human race that even now there is doubt as to whether all of it can be discharged fully before the end of the present age, even taking into account the suffering and pain which millions will experience during the time of chaos, turmoil and war which soon will engulf the planet. But the purpose of this time of trouble upon the earth—which we will return to at a later point in this treatise—is much more complex than merely the discharging of racial Karma, since it is one of the five pivotal experiences of the human race, and is expected to produce a resurgence of spirituality, dedication and brotherly love the like of which no other race on any other planet in the galaxy has ever experienced.

It can thus be seen that the experiences of pain and suffering which all men pass through, whether of a physical, emotional or mental nature, are of deep significance to the spiritual progress of the race, and indeed are absolutely essential if there is to be any hope that the mountain of spiritual achievement can be scaled. For in a very real sense, man is on a pilgrimage which is just like the scaling of a mountain. The summit is his goal, but the way is hard, the dangers are many and the temptations to rest and to cease trying are strong. He carries a burden on his back which weighs him down at every step: the burden of his negative Karma. Yet with each experience of pain or suffering the burden grows smaller and his step becomes lighter. Is it any wonder that souls who are between lives long for the opportunity to be incarnated again and to pass through the suffering which only the earth plane can dispense! The soul in that condition sees clearly the burden it carries and desires above all else to be rid of it.

We spoke of minor exceptions to the normal discharge of Karma, which ordinarily is taken away by experiences of pain and suffering on the part of him who was responsible for the actions giving rise to the negative Karma. There are two kinds of circumstance in which the setting aside of Karma can be accomplished by someone other than the owner of the Karma. The first usually occurs when the accumulation of the negative Karma was done in full knowledge of the Karmic law, and in the form of a sacrifice for others, in order that the others would be spared the necessity of doing the actions which would cause negative Karma to be generated.

An example can be taken from the middle Atlantean period. At a time more than 200,000 years ago, the human race had achieved a level of scientific accomplishment fully the equal of that found in the present day. The techniques of atomic fusion and fission had been mastered, the inert gas technology was used extensively for flight and for the generation of limitless amounts of free energy, and the communication techniques employed were even in advance of those used today.

In that long-distant period, mankind was threatened by a strange life-form which had developed on the planet, and which threatened to take over so much of the land area that there would eventually be no space left for the human species. The life-form in question was a kind of immense thought-form that was able to materialize itself into matter due to the conditions then prevailing. Hundreds of these huge masses of living tissue were abroad upon the earth, and were obliged to consume great quantities of vegetable life in order to maintain themselves. They can be visualized as mountainous but formless creatures, some over 1/2 mile in length, sprawled upon the land, moving slowly, devouring all of the plants and trees in their path, leaving behind a terrain stripped right down to the bare sub-rock, with nothing left alive upon it.

Men understood then that it was the beautiful canopy of trees on the planet which was primarily responsible for maintaining the oxygen content of the atmosphere, and that without the trees, the oxygen in the air would rapidly become depleted. It was feared that the immense animal forms, battening continuously upon the forests and woods, would eventually pose a threat to the oxygen supply, and it was decided that something had to be done to remove the danger, in order to preserve the many other life-forms then on the planet, including the human species. A desperate solution seemed the only way, namely to kill off the giant creatures by the use of atomic explosions detonated alongside them.

Although mankind then understood the principle of atomic fusion and fission, the technique had never previously been used to generate a chain-reaction explosion. The only prior use had been under highly controlled conditions such as in the present day nuclear power plants. Because there had been no previous experience with the explosive reaction at the atomic level, it was not possible to estimate just how great an explosive force a given amount of radioactive material would generate, nor how much radioactive residue would be left behind. It was desired to avoid any preliminary testing of the nuclear explosive technique because there was evidence that the creatures were highly adaptive to antagonistic conditions and it was feared that even remote testing would alert them to the danger and bring about adaptive changes which would allow the animals to survive the blasts that were planned.

In order to ensure the complete disintegration of these immense forms, the explosive devices were deliberately made very large, despite the danger that this might pose in terms of excessive shock to the earth's body and in terms of radioactive waste.

Men at that time understood the full meaning of the Karmic Law, and they knew that the deliberate destruction of these gigantic life-forms, even though primitive and without the capacity for rational thought, would bring much Karma upon the human race generally, and especially heavy burdens upon the individuals who would have to locate and detonate the atomic devices. Naturally, no one wished to be in these pivotal positions because of the Karmic load that was certain to result when the creatures were destroyed. But there were a few individuals whose love for their brothers was great enough to motivate them to volunteer for the key positions in the operation, and it was on these few that the greater part of the Karma descended.

To the great chagrin of almost all men then on the earth, the atomic explosions not only disintegrated the huge animals, but in addition simultaneously destroyed virtually all of the lifeforms living within a radius of 100 miles from each explosion. This would have been bad enough, but within two days after the explosions the earth's crust, weakened by the horrendous shock waves it had taken, began to shift and buckle at locations of weakness. One of these weak areas ran through Atlantis itself, and when the earthquakes and flooding finally subsided, it was found that fully one fifth of the Atlantean continent had been submerged, and that more than a third of her population had been destroyed.

The Karmic burden upon those who had volunteered for the key positions in the project was suddenly far greater than could have been imagined beforehand. Some of the volunteers could not bear the thought of the destruction that their actions had caused, and they took their own lives. Others went mad. A few withstood the terrible knowledge of what they had done, but these were never again as they had been before, and in all of their subsequent lives they have been driven to seek ways to make restitution for the great destruction for which they had been responsible. Many of these souls are today upon the earth, living lives of sacrifice for their brothers. Several of the great example-lives that have been lived, such as Ghandi and Schweitzer, were in part an attempt to undo the Karma that had arisen in that terrible time of destruction.

We have no wish to be thought of as story-weavers. The tale just outlined was primarily to show that there can be situations in which the noblest souls voluntarily perform acts which are certain to result in negative Karma, and also to disclose the principle circumstance under which that Karma can be lifted from the shoulders upon which it rests. Precisely this is what took place for those few who had volunteered out of compassion for their brothers. In saying that the Karma was lifted, we are not implying that it was annulled. Karma can never be annulled or obliterated except by being discharged through the physical body of some being. In the case in question, a number of very great entities, far beyond man in grandeur and spiritual essence, agreed to share the Karma that had befallen the men who had filled the key positions. As a result it has not been necessary for these individuals to suffer as they might have had to.

The decision to allow the Karma to be transferred was the responsibility of the Lords of Karma. If they had denied the request of the great entities who had volunteered to take the Karma, then the key men in the project would have had to assume it all themselves. It is quite likely that the attempt to set aside such a great Karmic burden would have spiritually destroyed them, and their souls would have ceased to exist as separate entities.

There is another instance in which a large segment of the racial Karma was discharged by an advanced entity, but in this case the entity was fully as human as the rest of mankind. We speak of the Master from Gallilee, Whose death upon the Cross lifted from each and every human soul a portion of the negative Karma which that soul was then carrying. There is thus a real truth behind the Biblical concept that Christ "died for our sins". The decision to allow the Master to take upon himself a part of humanity's Karmic burden was beyond the province of the Lords of Karma, since at the time of the suffering on the Cross, the Christ Spirit or Divine Logos would be in the body along with the spirit of the man Jesus. Thus, the Christ Spirit itself was also responsible for relieving man of some of his Karmic burden.

Both of the above instances belong to the same category, in

which for special reasons an advanced entity takes upon itself a part of the Karmic burden of one or more less advanced souls.

The second category, and the only other exception to the general rule, relates to instances where the love between two human souls is so great that one of them wishes to share the Karma of the other, in order to lighten the burden which the other carries. Requests of this kind are not often granted, and when they are it is usually because the one offering to share the Karmic burden of the other has distinguished himself by many acts of selfless devotion to his brothers, and thus acquires a stronger voice in the higher councils.

The recounting of the time of destruction in the middle-Atlantean period has served also to outline another of the five pivotal experiences of the race upon this planet. Along with the Tribulation, the Flood, the Temptation and the Transformation, it helps make up the Great Pentacle, as it is called.

The number 5 has immense significance for the human race, not only in designating the Great Pentacle of pivotal experiences, but also in identifying numerous special structures and symbols which have played significant roles in man's history.

One example is that of the Great Pyramid of Gizeh which is a structure far more holy than any temple ever to have been erected in the earth. It was built on the direct command of the Creator-God Himself, and embodies within itself an absolutely accurate prognostication of the entire time period from the era of Moses through to the end of the thousand years of glory to follow the Tribulation.

The pyramid shape is of course the architectural representation of the number 5, for it is a form with 5 corners. However the symbolism of the structure goes far deeper than this. Upon the earth the pyramid rests as a square, a four-cornered figure. The number 4 has always symbolized the earth plane, with its limitations, its shortages, its incitement to rivalry, aggression and warfare. Those who are attuned to the number 4 are continuously at odds with the environment and people around them. They find that others "rub them the wrong way" and the impression tends to be mutual. It is not by accident that the square or rectangle is the most favoured geometric form for the dividing up of property, farmland and the like, for the concept of possession of land is directly aligned with the rivalry and separative aspects of the number 4.

But in the pyramid, a further point is added at the peak, bringing the total number of corners to 5. The addition of the peak also completes 4 triangles, and it is well understood in occultism that the triangle represents the deep underlying spiritual truths that are available to man, if he were but to open his eyes to them. The triangle denotes the three-fold nature of man himself—mental, emotional and physical—and can be shown to correspond to a like division in all creatures that are "made in the image of the Creator", since in the Great God of All That Is, there is also found a three-fold manifestation. This is designated in the Christian Theology as God the Father (corresponding to Will, Creativity and the physical body), God the Son (which is the Divine Love or Christ Spirit) and God the Holy Ghost (the mental facet of God).

Much more will be said about the meaning of numbers at a later point in this work, but first it is desired to return to the Great Pentacle of racial experiences, and to describe another of them in greater detail.

We have identified the Great Pentacle as comprising the Temptation, the Flood, the Destruction (of the great animals), the Tribulation and the Transformation. This list is given in correct sequence of time. The first three events are in the past, the Tribulation is currently under way, and the Transformation will occur after the one-thousand year period of glory to follow the present time of chaos.

Our attention is now upon the first of these events, referred to in this treatise as the Temptation. There are scattered records of this era yet remaining, although nothing was written down during the actual period of the Temptation. All extant records were given by direct revelation at a time much later than that of the events themselves.

In the Judeo-Christian Bible, fragmented references are found to a time when the "Sons of God looked upon the Daughters of the Men", and scholars have been at a loss to interpret this passage meaningfully. The best recounting of the time in question occurs in the Book of Enoch, but the latter work was rejected by the early churchmen when deciding what the Bible would contain.

Briefly, the story is as follows. Man was created in human form some 10 million years before the present and in his initial state did not age and die as now. If he had done so, the spark of life within him would have been extinguished as a separate entity, and would have been reabsorbed back into the body of God, to await a subsequent projection in a different form. Man had no "soul" in the sense of a continuing "spark" capable of surviving the disintegration of the physical body.

Men at that early period were not differentiated sexually. Each entity included both male and female characteristics in roughly equal proportion. Life then was like that of an innocent child. The laws of Creation were universally and instinctively obeyed, because no temptation had arisen to act in any different manner. This period of innocence is represented symbolically in Genesis by the Garden of Eden. Adam, before Eve was formed from one of his own ribs, was the symbol of the hermaphrodite human, having both sexes in the one body. After a sufficient period of acclimatization to earth's conditions, it was decided by the entities who had been given charge of the human group that the next phase had to be initiated.

It must be fully understood here that at no time was the "human experiment" merely left to develop aimlessly on its own. A definite plan had been prepared even prior to the first breathing of mankind on the planet, and that plan has been followed precisely through all of the vicissitudes of fortune and disaster that the race has experienced.

Much of the plan is beyond man's mind to grasp at present. Parts of it must remain hidden for a while yet. But we are permitted to sketch the broad lines of the overall project in order that a few who read this text will be allowed to come to a deeper understanding of the position of humanity in the Cosmos.

We will begin by pointing out that, out of all the myriads of life-strewn planets in this vast Galaxy, the concept of "emotionalism" is known only on the earth. Only here, on what many extra-terrestrial races regard as a God-neglected bit of cosmic dust whose inhabitants are so unevolved as to be hardly worth coming to observe, do the notions of hate, fear, human love, greed and pity have any meaning at all. In all the vastness of this star-strewn Galaxy, no other race is able to grasp fully the meaning of these terms.

What is it, then, that has set the human race so apart from their cousins on other planets? The answer lies in the Great Plan for humanity which we have mentioned earlier. The entities who guide the affairs of planetary civilizations (from a far loftier plane in spiritual terms) had noted that the basic emphasis in all of the developed races was that of the *mental* side of the triangle. All of the other group evolutions had progressed by virtue of the mental *understanding* of God's laws. For example, in the advanced galactic races, no harm is ever deliberately done to any other living creature, but the restraint is due to an *understanding* of the Karmic Law which we have explained earlier, and is not the result of a feeling of *love* or *reverence* for the other creatures. These galactic groups comprehend the concept of God's Love with their minds, and know that it is by virtue of this Divine Love that they live and move and have their being, but they do not echo back a returned "feeling" of love toward the Creator, because their evolution has been such as to exclude the possibility of developing such a feeling.

Because of this situation, the great entities who direct the evolution of planetary races decided that there should be at least one civilization which would manifest the Divine Love facet at the "level of man" (which is the same level as that of the other galactic races we have described), and which would be eventually in a position to show the other, more mentally oriented races what this Love could accomplish.

The human race was asked whether it would accept the challenge of manifesting the Divine Love at the level of man, and agreed to the proposal. It was known full well that the way would not be easy, that the pitfalls would be many and that the self-inflicted suffering among the human group would be great, but the challenge was taken up and the program was begun.

All of the emotions of fear, hate, greed, pity, human love

and the rest are merely lopsided, narrow or twisted forms of the Love which the Creator has for all of His creatures: i.e. the Divine Love or Christ Spirit. It was decided that the only way for humanity to arrive finally at the highest manifestation of the Christ Love was to drag itself relentlessly through all of Love's perversions and contortions, to taste every negative and unholy feeling that could possibly be generated, and in the end to purify the body of emotion-experience that it would have collected, by passing through an extreme testing period during which the only apparent way to save oneself from obliteration would be to cast oneself on the loving mercy of God and pray for salvation.

It was thought that if the time of trial could be cleverly enough prepared, then the result would be an outshining of love and brotherhood on a scale so vast as to dumbfound the skeptical galactic races who have all along doubted the workability of the plan, and in the process teach them something about the Love of God that they could not possibly learn in any other way. It is essential not only for humanity but also for the other civilizations to learn something about the Love side of the Triangle of Being, for otherwise the highest crags of the mountain of spiritual light cannot be scaled. Thus the experiment upon this bit of cosmic dust, as they think of it, is for their benefit as well, and all higher entities who wish to see God's Creation unfold toward ever greater outflowerings of spirituality and light work and pray continuously for the success of the human race—especially now as the shadows of the Great Tribulation lengthen upon the planet.

Before returning to trace the story of the Temptation, one more facet of the Great Plan for the human race should be sketched.

In the symbolism of the material world, it is well understood that the sea corresponds to the emotion/feeling side of man. Water is ever the symbol of emotions, in dreams and in other forms of communication. The water which covers the earth over all but 1/4 of its surface is a distinct rarity in this galaxy. Very few other inhabited planets have atmospheric conditions which permit water to exist in liquid form, and those that do have but puny reservoirs of the liquid, not comparable in any way to the magnificent seas and oceans of the earth.

In the common subconscious level shared by all human beings, it is recognized that the sea represents the emotional side of the triangle—that which when purified will shine forth as the human equivalent of God's Divine Love. Through incarnation after incarnation, man seeks ever the experience of the sea. Much of his history has been lived on the oceans. The great cities of the earth are, with few exceptions, ports and harbours. Men seek instinctively the solace and calm which only the sea can provide.

But she has her darker side as well. Few humans have not, in some incarnation, been deprived of a loved one or of their own lives by the fury of the sea. Her treachery is known to all mariners. Her dangers are the watchword of all who sail upon her bosom.

And yet men return again and again to the sea, to sail her or to live beside her. She is like a magnet, attracting men life after life through her siren-song of proferred peace and solace.

The spell of the sea is easy to understand when it is realized that all humans know in their hearts that it is the emotional side of their natures that must eventually be made to flower, and recognize in the sea the perfect reflection of human emotions. Her treachery, her beauty, her seductiveness, her howling storms, her calm serenity—these all are found within man's own emotional nature. In living his life tied to the sea, man perceives outside of himself a perfect representation of that which lies within. So long as man continues to allow his emotional side to storm and to destroy, so long will it be necessary for the sea to do the same. The great hope of those who planned this partnership between mankind and the sea is that the outer experiences of the sea's negative side will allow man to recognize his own emotional negativity and to seek to purify it.

We now take up the story of the Temptation at a point when it had been decided that the era of innocence had run its course, that the human race had acclimatized sufficiently to earth's conditions, and that the next step of the plan should not be longer delayed.

In order to prepare the race for the Temptation, it was essential that the hermaphroditic individuals be, in effect, divided into their male and female halves. Bear in mind that conditions on the earth at that time were nothing like those present now. Today such a separation is incomprehensible due to the solidity and density of all matter on the earth. However, in that early epoch, all substance on the earth plane was of a much finer and more easily altered form. It was not in any way difficult to accomplish the kind of division we are discussing as far as the physical vehicles were concerned. Since man at that time possessed no higher vehicle and nothing corresponding to a soul or "eternal essence", the entities who undertook to arrange the great division into sexes had a relatively simple task before them.

The actual time during which the race underwent this sexual division lasted several hundred thousand years, with some individuals volunteering for the procedure early, and others delaying. None were forced to undergo the division.

The attraction toward the offered procedure was simple: it was explained that after the division had taken place, each half would then be a complete separate consciousness and that the two parts would be to each other as permanent mates. It was also explained that the reunion of the two halves in the sexual act would give to each a joy greater than any that had been known hiterto (hence the bliss that is yet experienced during the act of sexual intercourse).

After the division had been completed for all humans, symbolized in Genesis as the making of Eve from Adam's rib, the time of childlike innocence continued for a further period which was short by comparison with the term prior to division. At length, it was felt that mankind could not be kept any longer from the next stage in its program, even though it was known that the events to follow would bring pain and suffering beyond anything yet experienced.

The actual temptation was spread over a considerable period of time. To understand this event fully, it is necessary to describe another group of entities, separate from humanity, who lived at a level of bliss and holiness unimaginable by the men of the earth.

In Genesis there are described *two* creations of man. In the first chapter man is said to have been created on the sixth day of the Creation Week. But in the second chapter another creation is described, this time with emphasis on the earthly nature of the creation ("... of the dust of the earth..."). The first description refers not to the human group but rather to an earlier race of "men" who were established in realms known as the astral planes. These planes are near to the earth but are of a material much finer than physical matter. The first men were created in two sexes initially, and were endowed with an eternal essence, or soul as it might now be called.

It was a part of the plan, not only for humanity (the second men) but also for these first men, that the earlier group was to be tempted into trying to lead the human beings away from the Laws of Creation to which everyone automatically adhered at the time.

In order to carry out the temptation of the first men, it was necessary to find one of their number who would volunteer to play the part of mischief-maker, and who would try to persuade as many as possible to interfere with the situation among humans on the earth.

The first men included a small number of very powerful beings, acting as leaders, and a much larger number of less powerful beings. Among the powerful leaders was one named Lucifer, a beautiful and shining entity of great wisdom and love. It was this entity who, because of his devotion to the will of still higher beings who carried out God's own will, volunteered to act as the seducer who would tempt others of the first men to try to interfere with the situation as it then was on the earth.

This matter is difficult to recount in earth language because of the subtleties of meaning that are required. It is especially difficult at this point because what then took place has no analogue in earth experience. The entity Lucifer allowed a part of himself to be removed and to become a separate "reflection" of himself. This might be compared to the relation between the conscious and subconscious minds of a single person, although the comparison is not very good. The "reflection" Lucifer then proceeded to instigate a turning away from the Laws of Creation to which his own brothers had till then faithfully adhered. One of these was an injunction not to interfere with the progress of any other group of entities, and another was to avoid mixing procreatively with any such other group.

The "reflection" Lucifer was able to persuade about a third of his brothers, both males and females, to join with him in an attempt to lead the human group into debauchery in the sense of procreative relations.

This Temptation of the humans actually took place by stages. The first stage was to suggest to the "mated" pairs of humans that they should try to have sexual union with humans other than their own mates, for the sake of variety. Many succumbed to this idea even though it brought much pain to the race at the emotional level. The feeling of rejection on the part of the mate passed over for another was particularly acute because it was, for all humans so treated, the very first wound to the heart that any had experienced.

The suggestion to introduce variety into the sexual experience was made easily to the human group, because at the time the first men had regular interchange with humanity for purposes of teaching and the setting of examples. Almost all of the first men had, since the earliest era of humanity upon the earth, regularly visited the planet, and much affection had grown up between the elder and the younger groups. It should be explained that the teaching, the setting of examples and even the affection were by no means against any of God's Laws. On the contrary, it was expected that the group with greater experience in higher planes would try to help and enlighten those who had not existed for as long a time.

Following the inducement to vary the sexual experience, it was an easy next step to suggest that the humans have sexual relations with the first men themselves. Here occurred the great transgression in terms of the Laws of Creation. In the Bible, the Temptation just mentioned is symbolized by the whisperings of the serpent in the Garden of Eden, although later in the same book there is a further reference to this time, when the "Sons of God looked upon the Daughters of Men and saw that they were fair".

It is not necessary to provide details of this cross-breeding period, beyond saying that there were indeed offspring of the sexual unions. The progeny included mutants, giants, bestial entities and others more man-like in form.

Because these poor creatures had one parent who was immortal and another who was not, there was doubt as to whether the creatures should themselves be given immortal status, a gift within the power of the entities who directed the evolution of planetary races.

A decision was made to provide the creatures with an eternal essence or soul, and simultaneously the same gift was extended to all of the humans.

The extension of the gift of soul to all humans is easily said, but it represents something of profound and inestimable importance to each human being. Without this gift, man would not have been able to arrive at the point where he now is, for with the gift of the soul came also the gift of death.

We are not playing with words when we describe death as a gift. It will be seen from the subsequent discussions that the passing from this plane to higher planes is an utterly essential phase for all human souls in terms of the learning process that has gone on since the time of the Temptation.

We wish to point out what may appear to be a contradiction in what we have recounted regarding the transgression of the Creator's Laws involving procreative intermixing between separate groups. We had earlier said that the human group have followed a definite plan from the beginning and this implies that even the "turning away" from the Laws of Creation was part of that plan, therefore how can it be a transgression? The solution to this riddle lies in understanding that there are different levels of laws applicable at the various planes of being. At the "level of man", which includes the first and second men described above, and also the numerous galactic races we have mentioned, the injunction not to interfere with each other and not to mix procreatively applies. But from the much higher level from which the destiny of the races of men is directed, it is possible to abrogate those laws, and even to use a transgression of those laws in order to promote further growth and learning at the level of man. This is precisely what took place in the story we have recounted.

To return to our discussion of death, it is essential to recall that prior to the time of the Transgression no death had taken place among the humans on the earth. The atmosphere and other energy conditions about the earth were such as to continuously renew all the living tissues of the human group, so that aging and decay were unknown. Few realize that even now such conditions could be restored on the earth by altering the constituents of the atmosphere and by changing the nature of man's thought and emotional habits. Much of the misery of illness and premature death among mankind today could be removed if men were simply to understand that their whole being, including the physical body, is deeply affected by thought and emotion; and that stressful emotions like hatred and resentment are just as corrosive to the body as the drinking of battery acid might be.

Thus the race had not had, at the epoch in question, any personal experience of death. (The animal kingdom however was just as it is today, with much cyclical birth and death, in which the animal souls were able to enter, leave and re-enter the earth plane with great ease. To the animal souls the reincarnational process presented no more of a problem than falling asleep and waking up.

Men of that time knew that the animals reincarnated continuously, not only because they were taught this truth by the first group of men, but also because man then had a much more highly developed psychic sense, and could literally see the animal souls leaving at death and arriving at birth.)

By the time the Temptation had run its course, after virtually all the humans had participated in the debauchery of crossmixing, it had become very clear to all who had taken part that they had literally befouled the universe for the sake of variety and pleasure. The evidence of this lay in the poor creatures that were born of the miscegenation. Almost without exception they were mutated, horrible to look at, and of extremely low vibration in terms of spirituality. Yet such was the universal reverence for all life at the time that the humans permitted these monsters to live freely among them, thus reminding men continuously of the turning away that had taken place.

The earlier men who came to tempt the humans were also responsible for planting the seeds of dissension among them. This was accomplished by passing out certain secrets relating to hypnotism and to universal laws (which would now be called magic because they are no longer understood) by which one human could influence or gain control over another. Many humans began to experiment with these dark teachings, and after a time there sprang up a whole philosophy, to which many adhered, which held that the pleasure and importance of the self of each human should be of greater importance to that person than the pleasure and importance of another, even the mate.

The latter concept does not sound strange to modern ears because man today is imbued with the idea that he has the right to seek first his own pleasure, wealth, happiness, etc., and that consideration for others should take second place. The right to life, liberty and happiness is even enshrined in the constitution of the United States as a fundamental prerogative of each individual, while the economic system adhered to by all western countries holds as sacrosanct the right of each individual to operate in his own interest and against that of others if need be.

We do not say that individual freedoms and rights are wrong, for they are not. We are merely pointing out that the selfishness which is rampant among all men today finds full support in the political and economic ideas that are the basis for western civilization, and that therefore one should not wonder at the fierceness with which most humans today would, if challenged, defend their right to be selfish.

In that long distant epoch, before the whisperings of the fallen first men, each human placed the group to which he belonged before his own interests. Especially did each man cherish the happiness of his mate ahead of his own. The idea of promoting self and the self's personal interests ahead of others was totally foreign to the thought patterns then existing, and indeed even the concept of the self as a separate individualized unit was unheard of.

Here we come to a crucial point, for one of the very important stages in the long pilgrimage of the human race has been that related to the development of *individuality*, the ability to see oneself as distinct and separate from the group, and as *worthy* in the sight of God.

As so often with the human race, it was realized that in order to come to the "middle way" regarding this question, in which individual self-worth would be recognized without infringing the freedoms and rights of others—and without denying the self-ness of the others—it would be necessary first to let the pendulum swing all the way to the opposite side from where it had started out: namely, to allow a full manifestation of self-assertiveness, selfishness, control of others, and so forth, in the hope that man would learn by himself, through the pain that such behaviour caused him, to moderate his attitudes and to again place the interests of others before his own. If this procedure could be made to work, then the result would be a happy blend of a strong self-image, self worth and individuality on the one hand, together with kindness and self-sacrifice on the other.

It is not hard to understand why so many of the later way-showers who came to the earth plane to teach their brothers, including Jesus of Nazareth, have insisted that the placing of the interests of others over those of the self is the surest path to Godliness. They were attempting to help restore the pendulum to a middle position, since man had by then accomplished quite enough in terms of individualizing the self.

Thus it can be realized that, even though the whisperings and seductions of the fallen first men relating to selfishness and egotism seemed to be something of a dark and unspiritual nature at the time (as it did to those of the first men who refused to participate), nonetheless in the great plan set by the higher entities who direct the destinies of planetary races it was essential that such turning away take place, or otherwise the necessary individuality and self-esteem of each human could not have been developed.

We have said that the gift of death was given along with the gift of the soul, and this is true. However for death actually to take place among the humans of that epoch, it would be necessary to change physical conditions on the earth and also to alter the constitution of the bodies which men then had. The first death to occur was that of a special man who was created after the Temptation. This man is he who is referred to as Adam in the Judeo-Christian Bible, and indeed that was his name. (We distinguish between the symbolic and the designative levels of the Adam story in the Scriptures.)

The creation of Adam as a new human (which was something that had not happened since the original breathing of man on the planet millions of years before) was not an isolated or chance event. On the contrary, it was part of a vast new phase in the plan for humanity, namely the reincarnational phase. It was decided that the immersion of men in the despicable practices of controlling others, selfishness and outright cruelty had to be ended, and that it was time for man to taste death so that he could take the first faltering steps into realms beyond the earth, which can only be entered when the physical body has been laid aside.

This new phase was of great complexity. As we have already pointed out in *The Nature of Reality*, the Reincarnation project involved sacrifices from several quarters. Firstly there was that of man, who volunteered to sacrifice the physical body and pass to higher planes of learning after death. Secondly there was an agreement by those of the first men who had not joined Lucifer, according to which they would act as guides and teachers of the human group until the material phase of humanity would terminate. Thirdly there was the shutting away of a large number of the first men who had disobeyed the Creator's Laws, with however some possibility for most of them to set aside the Karma they had accumulated during the Temptation by passing through experiences of suffering on the material plane. Finally there was a contribution from the Creator Himself, who projected from the Divine Love portion of the Trinity a human spark who would be the soul of the first mortal man, Adam. There was also an agreement that this special soul would be put through many purifying life experiences during the reincarnational project, and then when the two great cosmic clocks rang the same hour, he would live a final incarnation, during three years of which the Christ Spirit or Divine Love principle would literally inhabit the physical body along with the human soul. This final incarnation was of course that of Jesus of Nazareth, which began just as the wheel of ancient Constellations became aligned with the astrological wheel of Zodiac signs.

We had said in our earlier book, *The Nature of Reality*, that the Karmic principle was also inaugurated at the beginning of the Reincarnational project, but this was a distortion in that first transmission, due to the incomplete grasp which the channel then had of Karmic law. The truth is that the process represented by the word Karma has continued from the very first tick of time for all creatures everywhere. However it did become possible, with the advent of the reincarnational scheme, to set aside more Karma more rapidly than was previously the case, because of the pain of parting which death brought.

Here then was the second major wound to the heart of man. Imagine the feeling of loss in one "twin soul" upon the death of his mate, who had literally been a part of him before the division, and who had been with him for time beyond memory.

It is perhaps becoming clear that the great overall plan we are describing was specifically designed to awaken the emotional nature in man through pain and loss that only the emotions could experience. It will be seen that this process has continued even to the present, and will find its greatest activity at the height of the Tribulation within only a few short years from the time of this dictation.

Returning now to the introduction of the death experience, it was part of the Reincarnational project that the man Adam would be so created physically that he would be the first to die and pass to the higher realms. In order to initiate the physical aging and decay process a change was made in the earth's atmosphere, involving the removal of almost all of the gaseous element Xenon which it then contained. It is Xenon, among the five inert gases, which is principally able, when properly excited, to produce a beam of energy of a special kind capable of sustaining and repairing living tissue of all kinds. The excitation of Xenon or any other inert gas is a simple process involving pressurizing the gas and then placing it in a strong magnetic field, as we have already explained in *The Nature of Reality*. The conditions then existing within earth's atmosphere involved enough pressure and sufficient magnetic flux (the earth's own magnetic field) to cause a low level excitation of the inert gases in the atmosphere and due to the large volume of the atmospheric reservoir even this low level produced a generalized Xenon energy flux capable of maintaining human tissues indefinitely.

However once the Xenon had been removed from the atmosphere with the assistance of advanced galactic civilizations of great technical accomplishment, the aging process began in all men. Because of the physical make-up of Adam, he was the first to reach the point of death, and thus was the way-shower to his brothers in terms of the higher (astral) realms, just as in a later incarnation he was the way-shower on earth for the age which has been called that of Pisces. This first death experience explains why Christ is referred to in Revelations as the "first-born of the dead".

As an aside, it may interest scientists to know that the efficacy of Xenon in terms of regenerating worn or damaged tissue remains to the present and any who cared to conduct the simple experiment involving pressure and magnetic flux would soon see that what we have revealed here is the truth.

The evil practices we have discussed earlier, arising from the teachings of the fallen angels (let us use the correct term from now on) were not extinguished upon the initiation of the Reincarnational project. Indeed many thousands of years elapsed between the death of Adam and the death of the last of the humans who were projected upon the earth in the beginning. This was due to the variations in physical make-up in the men of the time, and also (even primarily) to the different thought and emotional patterns of individuals. Those who harboured resentment and hatred decayed early, while those who tried to practice forgiveness and kindness lasted much longer. In a general way the same is true today, in the sense that negative emotions and feelings are translated directly into physical symptoms. The worse the negativity of the emotions, the greater the severity of the physical affliction. If man but knew how much physical damage he was inflicting upon himself through negative emotions, he would forthwith cease to feel and think in harmful ways.

At length all who had initially been breathed forth upon the earth were gone, their places taken by new generations of men who had emerged only as the Reincarnation project got under way.

In that early time, there were several ways of creating new bodies for the reincarnation of souls who had previously died. One of these was that of the present day, in which a genetic code is established in the womb of the female, and the soul wishing to reincarnate moulds and forms the developing body by the force of will and visualization from the higher plane. Then, at birth, the soul becomes tied to the new physical vehicle.

Another means of producing a physical body was simply for the incarnating soul to literally precipitate the new vehicle from the aethers of space by a supreme exercise of concentration, in "sanctified" locations reserved for this purpose. These locations later became the "temples" in which man worshipped, although this was after it ceased to be possible to precipitate matter from the aether by concentrated thought. Hence there is a kind of equivalence of function between the womb of the female and the sanctified location or temple, and it is perhaps not surprising that in occult understanding it is the physical body of man that is his true temple, as it has always been.

A final procedure was for a number of individuals to join together in the thought-projection of a physical vehicle for another soul who was not capable of the necessary degree of concentration. This latter method came to be more and more used as conditions in the earth became more solid or dense, since the altering conditions were making it harder and harder for individual souls to precipitate bodies by themselves.

At last, the earth conditions became such that it was no longer possible to use thought alone to create bodies, which meant that the present normal method of foetal development in the womb was the only remaining alternative.

Yet this too was part of the great plan for mankind. Physical birth from the womb of a woman was then, as it is now, an emotional experience of great depth, far more so than occurred when the body was simply precipitated by concentrated thought. It can be realized that here is another of the emotional promptings that the great plan was designed to bring about, in order to awaken fully the emotional side of the human race.

After all of the men initially created had passed through the gateway of death, it was decided that certain of the mutated life forms arising at the time of the Temptation had to be destroyed, because they too were giving birth in the normal foetal manner and thus were passing on distorted genetic codes not capable of forming physical vehicles suitable for advancing souls to inhabit. It was also felt that the time had come to make the first great impact upon the tiny emotional flames that had been encouraged to burn within the hearts of men by the previous emotional experiences, through a stark demonstration of the power of emotionalism when its negative side was uncontrolled. This was to be done symbolically, by having the sea flood the inhabited land areas, since the waters of the ocean were recognized at the subconscious level of man as representing the wells of emotional experience.

The experience of drowning is of deep symbolic meaning for the human race. All souls have lost at least one life in this manner, and many have drowned in several experiences on the earth plane.

To understand the symbolic level of drowning, it is first necessary to realize that the unconscious symbolism implanted in man is far more complex than we have thus far described. The air which man breathes, for example, is symbolically related to the mental or intellectual side of the triangle. Similarly the earth under one's feet corresponds to the physical body and the carnal level of experience.

When a person loses his life by drowning, there is portrayed in vivid outline for the soul a symbolic representation of what happens when the emotional side is allowed to run wild and overcome the mind, in the sense of intellectual or rational thought. It must be understood that, while mankind is intended to manifest the Divine Love at the human level, it has never been expected that the emotional side would drown out or nullify the life of the mind. Indeed, it is just as necessary for man to develop the mind and the *control* of the thought process as it is for any other galactic race. Moreover it was expected that the constant pricking of the emotional side into life would occasionally lead to circumstances in which the thought processes were at the mercy of the negative emotions, and it was this danger that had to be represented symbolically to the race in the experience of the Flood.

Hence the Flood, the second of the pivotal racial experiences making up the Great Pentacle, was of the deepest significance to the race. Only during the Tribulation now in progress will men be presented with an equivalent panorama of destruction and loss. The difference between the two experiences relates to the apparent source of the destruction. In the Flood, man saw the source as other than himself, since at the conscious level he did not realize that he himself had been responsible for the inundation. Specifically the morass of negative emotions which man had built up in the aethers of space over the millenia prior to the Flood were simply allowed to precipitate into material form as water. There had been so much of this negativity that almost all of the land then inhabited was covered by the resulting water.

During the later Destruction in Atlantis, although this did not cause as widespread a loss as the Flood, man did realize that he had been responsible. However the degree of destruction which resulted was unintentional and was not expected, and therefore the feeling of guilt was less than might have been the case if man had deliberately set out to wreak havoc upon the earth and the lifeforms she harbors.

In the Tribulation now in progress, man will see more clearly than ever before the direct link between his own inner condition and the external circumstances that result. It is this supreme lesson—that what man is like *within* directly affects the world around him—that these three progressive experiences were meant to teach. Thus the first, that of the Flood, implanted the lesson only at the unconscious level, since it did not appear to the conscious mind of the race that their own inner state was the source of the inundation. The second experience, the Destruction in Atlantis, showed more clearly man's responsibility for external conditions although again it was not evident that man's own inner processes had been responsible for the inherent weakness in the earth's crust and even for the presence of the huge formless animals that threatened his existence. The third and last phase of the lesson, now being acted out in the great Tribulation, will make it abundantly clear to all who experience the destruction and chaos about to befall the earth, that man and man alone is the author of all evil which besets him, and conversely that he can with effort transmute any negative external circumstance into a positive one simply by purifying himself of negativity. This is the hidden meaning of the Scriptural admonition: "seek ye first the Kingdom of Heaven, and all else will be added unto you".

During the Flood, only a smattering of humanity survived. The Adamic genetic strain was preserved in the family of the patriarch who has been called Noah, though it must be understood that he saved far more people than his own immediate family from the hungry waters. The ship he constructed held more than one hundred humans, together with certain specific animal life-forms which he had been told by revelation to collect in the boat. By no means did he take two of each species, for the boat was not big enough to harbor so many animals. The species selected were those that were in danger of extinction from the Flood and numbered only about 200, mostly small life-forms.

Of course, there were locations on the earth, especially the higher elevations and mountainous regions, which were not submerged. The humans living in these regions were nonetheless subjected to the continuous downpour for over a month, and much erosion, landslide activity and the loss of important crops ensued in these locations, bringing a great deal of hardship.

In the Flood experience all of the mutated life-forms resulting from the cross-mixing of humans and angels were destroyed, save one. The exception was a humanoid creature of short stature, powerfully built but of low intelligence compared to the normal humans. It was decided that this genetic strain would be ideal as a vehicle for those human souls who had lost ground spiritually throughout previous life-experiences, because it would suit them vibrationally, and moreover the experience of an unevolved soul finding itself in an unevolved physical body would, it was hoped, bring home to that soul the seriousness of the downward path it had been treading.

The plan was that these creatures, whom we shall call the Workers, were to live in association with the more evolved humans in the cities and towns, and to carry out tasks of manual labor in an atmosphere of kindness and consideration on the part of those more advanced, so that the Workers would learn kindness by observation, the value of effort by experience, and the importance of soul-evolution through the constant symbol of their own backwardness which their bodies constituted.

Occasionally some of the Workers left the inhabited cities and attempted to live on their own, away from the civilized areas. This they were permitted to do, for they were free to choose their path in life. But almost invariably these settlements disintegrated due to the backwardness and selfishness of the souls inhabiting the Worker bodies, and they descended eventually to the level of savages. As such, they did not take care to cremate their bodies after death, and occasional remains of these bodies have been found in modern times. It is these poor creatures who have been identified by anthropologists as Neanderthal man and other designations. By no means were they ever the progenitors of any humans alive today.

The Worker group as a whole remained in association with the more evolved humans for several hundred thousand years, right up to the last destruction of Atlantis only about 12,000 years ago. Then, in that final Atlantean disaster, all were destroyed.

Having now described the three parts of the Great Pentacle which have already taken place, it is fitting to go back over certain specific epochs of man's history and fill in more detail, in order to provide a more rounded view of the past of the race.

It might be thought, from the emphasis on destruction in the foregoing portion, that all of man's history is nothing but a sad tale of chaos, holocaust, and ruin. This would be far from the truth, for man's time on this planet has included truly golden ages of light and love, when the truth of the spirit flowered and all who lived in the earth were happy. These epochs took place even after the beginning of the Reincarnational project, despite the on-going necessity to serve out the Karma that had been accumulated in prior experiences.

One of the most advanced times upon the earth took place just before the sinking of the great Continent of Lemuria in the Pacific Ocean some 26,000 years ago. This was a period during which there was a great deal of contact between the human race and other galactic groups of greater advancement, both technically and spiritually.

There were scattered colonies of the galactic visitors on the earth in that epoch, and one of the most marvellous was that at what is now called Tiahuanaco. At the time, Tiahuanaco was a port city and lay beside the entrance to a canal which cut across the South American Continent at the present latitude of the Amazon river. Indeed the Amazon valley is what remains of that waterway.

In Tiahuanaco lived members of an advanced race from a planet circling a relatively nearby star in the constellation Draco. These colonists were about seven feet in height, were in two sexes, and resembled present-day man very closely except for their ear and hand configurations. The hand had only three fingers and a thumb, and the ear was rather pointed. Aside from these characteristics and a slightly greenish tint to the skin, the colonists would have been taken simply for very tall human beings.

In Tiahuanaco also lived a large number of the Workers which we have already described. This latter group did the manual labor, a certain amount of construction, and so forth. They were not slaves by any means. They were free to leave at any time, but those in Tiahuanaco had elected to stay and work for their living, because they understood consciously that the experience of proximity to the advanced galactic race would be extremely beneficial in terms of spiritual progress.

All travel of a mechanized nature was underground in Tiahuanaco, somewhat akin to present-day subways. On the surface were dwellings and official buildings. The Workers were employed to carry the galactic colonists about on the equivalent of litters, a practice which was repugnant to most of the colonists but which they participated in because they knew that it was only through service to those more advanced that there could be any hope for spiritual progress among the Worker race.

There stands today in Tiahuanaco, a huge monolith called the Gate of the Sun. It contains heiroglyphs carved into the rock, which have defied all attempts to translate them. The difficulty of translation is not because the glyphs are worn or because they were applied in some abstruse code. The problem is simply that the thought categories of those attempting the translation did not embrace the possibility that the message might have been for a galactic race other than human beings. If they had hit upon this concept, the translators would have quickly seen that the message runs something along the following lines:

"Sons and daughters of the light, believe in yourselves, and believing, reach out to the children of the darkness whom you have come to teach and uplift. Choose your words always within the compass of their understanding.

The earth is the home of a race destined for greatness within the cosmos. Your task is to seek ways to encourage them in the battle for individuality and light.

The worker race lives among you for the benefit of the souls within them, who have lost ground spiritually over the aeons of time that are now the past. Treat them always with gentle love and patience, for their struggle is greater than yours. They are forging a new growth of the spirit in the crucible of their toil and their suffering.

The humans of higher evolvement are also under your care. Do not think of them as backward or slow, for they have come from the God of All That Is, as you have, and their destiny is to return, as is yours. They sail upon the seas of this planet as you have traversed the aethers of space. Their bravery and courage are a match for your own.

As to the budding Greek civilization, remember that they hunger in the soul for the gifts of language, history and writing. In them especially, the written word lies folded as a flower, waiting to open in splendour. Seek to foster that unfoldment to the fullest bloom, for their language is to be a mighty voice across the ages to come, and the history they write will ripen the race to its maturity."

It is a message of great spirituality, intended for eyes that are past the sufferings and narrowness of the human race as it is today; eyes that have seen so much of the miraculous creation of God that they could never conceive of the possibility of bringing harm to any creature on any planet.

The purpose for the colony at Tiahuanaco was two-fold. Firstly it was to serve as a base from which the human race could be studied, so that later during the third major period of chaos, namely the great Tribulation presently in progress, the visitors and observers from other star systems could prepare themselves to help mankind when the hour grew to its darkest point. The second purpose was to offer spiritual teaching to the human race, and many of the visitors undertook journeys to far parts of the earth, in order to spread their higher understanding of God's laws. These entities have passed into legends and folk-stories, particularly in South and Central America, for they uplifted the hearts and minds of countless thousands of their human cousins. These odysseys have been the greatest gift that the galactic races have thus far made to the human race, although in the time to come the help and teaching of man's galactic cousins will swell to a great inpouring of light and truth, that will dwarf the efforts put forth during the Tiahuanacan epoch.

The time during which the galactic race maintained a colony at Tiahuanaco extended over several hundred years. It was known to all of the extra-terrestrial observers at a point prior to establishing the Tiahuanacan colony that a time of natural upheaval, destruction and mountain-building was planned by those who guided the destiny of the earth from a higher plane, and it was desired to implant some form of higher teaching among men before the chaos which the upheavals would bring, so that they would have available spiritual ideas and concepts to which they could turn for understanding when the destruction took place.

Just before the first of the upheavals, the colonists at Tiahuanaco and elsewhere left the earth in their vehicles, and they remained off the surface for the seven years of destruction that ensued. During this period, the Andes and Rocky mountain chains were created, and simultaneously the continent of Lemuria in the mid-Pacific Ocean sank beneath the waters. Much damage was also done to Atlantis in the Atlantic Ocean.

The primary cause of the upheavals and the subsidence of land was the contraction of the earth's crust, due to the venting of vast underground gas chambers which were located under several continents, principally Lemuria. These chambers were filled with combustible gases, and when the latter mixed with the oxygen of the air there arose gigantic conflagrations which could be seen for hundreds of miles. Large amounts of oxygen in the air were consumed in these immense fires, and as a result certain weaker life-forms perished. Man's own lung-capacity increased through natural selection after this destruction, in order to accommodate the race to the smaller oxygen content in the air.

We have given details of this time of destruction for several purposes, one of which is to explain that the process of natural selection is a perfectly sound principle that the early anthropologists correctly recognized. Although the *origin* of the human species is other than that which is now believed by science, nonetheless the metabolism, the chemistry and even the physical make-up of man has been deliberately altered countless times in his history in order to bring about changes that were thought desirable in the light of his spiritual growth. These alterations occurred by natural selection.

Let us elaborate further by revealing more about the increased lung capacity that was created by decreasing the oxygen content of the atmosphere during the time of mountain-building and crustal contraction 26,000 years ago.

Firstly, it is incorrect to imagine that the energy which drives the physical body of man comes from the food he eats. This is one of the major misconceptions in the world today, in spite of the fact that many pioneers of fruit-diets, fasting and so forth have shown conclusively that man can live quite well on practically no food at all, with no diminution of energy (quite the contrary, as all who have tried it have found).

The energy of man's body must come from a far more subtle and refined source than that of carbohydrate molecules, as is now believed. The life process in man does not exist at the mere chemical level, otherwise man would be nothing more than a beaker in which reactive chemicals were mixed, and with no more "life", intelligence or spirit than would be found in such a beaker. When the chemical reaction had run its course, the beaker would be quite still, lifeless, empty, and the same in the case of the human being.

No, the force that drives the human machine is not chemical, but aetheric. The aether is a form of all-embracing substance more rarified than the subtlest of man's chemicals, and indeed is the "stuff" from which all the elements known to science are precipitated, just as water droplets can be precipitated from water vapour in the air.

Mixed with the aether which fills all of man's three-dimensional space (even between the protons and electrons of matter in what science considers to be "empty" space) is a substance which we shall call *prana*, using the eastern word for life-energy. Indeed, the eastern religions know of this miraculous substance and understand quite well its role in supporting the "life" of man.

When the human body breathes air into the lungs, the prana within the aetheric counterpart of the air is taken into the aetheric counterpart of the body, and is then transformed into the various energies that one uses in everyday life: mental energy, emotional energy and physical energy.

The oxygen which is taken into the blood via the lungs of course plays a part in the metabolism, but it is only a minor role compared to the importance of the intake of prana.

Now, before the mountain-building epoch 26,000 years ago, man's lung capacity was significantly smaller than it is today, and it was thought that the then correspondingly smaller intake of the vital prana would not give sufficient energy to the body to match the needs of the more advanced soul-level that man was shortly expected to attain. The greater the advancement spiritually, the greater the soul-energy, and the larger the physical body must be to match that soul-energy with its own energy.

Thus, the process of natural selection in the millennia after the destruction of 26,000 years ago brought about a 30% increase in man's lung capacity. At the same time it broadened his shoulders (to accommodate the greater lung size). This larger shoulder width was also of importance symbolically, and to understand why, it will be necessary to digress briefly, in order to teach something of the body symbolism which, though understood by all men subconsciously, is not yet recognized at the conscious level.

The shape and construction of the human form is not merely an accident of nature with no purpose beyond adaptation to surrounding conditions. All of the major features of the human body represent some characteristic at either the *soul* level or the *personality* level.

Since many readers are unfamiliar with this two-fold nature of man, it would be well first to explain the dichotomy in greater detail before touching on the symbolic meanings of the main body features.

We have already shown that man has a higher part or eternal essence, sometimes called the soul. To avoid confusion in later books from this source, we will call this essence the "higher self", as contrasted with the personality level or "lower self".

Each of these "selves" has a three-fold nature, in keeping with the triangular symbolism discussed earlier in this book. In the lower self or everyday personality, there are the mental, emotional and physical levels. These are matched in the higher self by three facets which will be called herein the Atmic, the Buddhic and the Brahmic.

The lower self has three bodies or "sheaths" corresponding to the three facets: the aetheric body responds to the mental vibrations; the astral body responds to emotional states; and the physical body is the seat of all earth-related sensation and carnality. In the higher self, the three facets named Atmic, Buddhic and Brahmic can be thought of as bodies or sheaths that correspond to the mental, emotional and physical respectively.

There is a beautiful symbolic diagram which shows all three bodies for both selves, and which is more ancient than any other of man's symbols. Begin by drawing a triangle of equal sides with the peak pointing up. This represents the higher self with its three facets. The upward pointing apex signifies that the higher self's attention is constantly on the spiritual light from above. Now draw another triangle below the first, also an equal-sided figure but with the point downwardly. This bottom triangle represents the lower self with its three-faceted make-up, and the downward pointing apex signifies that the attention of the lower self or personality is downwardly toward things of the earth, practical considerations, etc.

These two triangles, representing the higher self and the lower self, may be thought of as joined by a multiplicity of energy paths connected between various parts of the two triangles like electric wires. Along these paths wisdom and energy from the higher self flow to the lower, and experience and knowledge from the lower flow up to the higher. It should be pointed out that the energy from the higher self which feeds into the lower self is not sufficient to "run the engine" of the personality, and must be supplemented by pranic force in the manner discussed earlier. However, when the energy and contact from the higher self is reduced or limited, the ability of the lower sheaths to extract energy from the aetheric prana is also curtailed, and weakness or illness can result. This is due to the fact that the soul energies from the higher self are like master-circuits that control all others. This may be compared to a controlling circuit in electronics which itself takes only a small amount of current, but which is able to turn on and off a much heavier current in the circuit which it controls.

The aim of the seeker after soul-advancement is to try to link the higher and lower selves together by the strongest possible energy paths, so that in effect the attitudes and wisdom of the higher become available to the conscious personality. Through perseverence and self-control this state of one-ness can be attained, and it is represented symbolically by drawing the two triangles one on top of the other. The result is of course the ancient symbol which has been utilized by the Jewish religion as the Star of David.

Moreover, the true significance of this beautiful geometric figure will explain the symbolic purpose served by water when it crystalizes as snow. Men have wondered for aeons why the snowflakes are six-pointed. Few have guessed that the phenomenon was meant to remind them ceaselessly of the goal of earth incarnation in terms of bringing the higher self and the lower self into one-ness with each other.

To return now to the question of the symbolic meaning of various parts of the human body, we will begin by pointing out the most obvious relationship, yet one which very few men have ever realized at the conscious level. We are referring to the nose. Man has an expression which, at the level from which this dictation is emanating, is considered highly amusing: "as plain as the nose on your face". If only its meaning symbolically were as plain as this expression suggests! But only a handful of men realize that the nose on the human face—and indeed the nose of *any animal*—bears a direct relation to the self-image and feeling of self-worth which that person (or animal) has.

We have pointed out earlier that one of the major tasks of man upon the earth has been to develop a concept of individuality, of the distinction between one man and another. In order to do this, it is essential to be happy with the self-picture which is formed through the individualization process, for otherwise there will be little impetus to manifest and expand that individuality.

The relation between the nose and the feeling of self-worth is a direct one. Body language in the sense we are discussing it was never meant to be obscure. If the nose is large, so is the self-image. If small, the same is true of the picture of the self. Consider a little child. Almost invariably infants and young children have very diminutive noses. The reason is now obvious: the self-image or feeling of self-worth in the small child is still in the process of developing. It is very much at the mercy of the attitudes which the parents have toward the child. If a parent treats a child in a way to suggest that the child is of little value or unloved, then the self-image of the child will be stunted in its growth. Such children when they grow up will have smaller noses than would have been the case had they been made to feel worthy, loved and happy with themselves.

Another fact should have been a clue to the meaning behind the nose. Doctors now know that, generally, the nose continues to grow throughout life. For the average person, the gradual enlargement of the nose is consonant with the (usually) improving self-image that the person has. Where a person does not improve the self-image, the nose does not grow.

Additional points can be made. In *The Nature of Reality*, we pointed out the identities of the advanced souls which now incarnate as horses, elephants and whales, all of which have quite large noses or nose-equivalents. Since these ensouling entities are of the highest level in terms of soul-progress, it is fitting (and indeed could not be otherwise) that the life-forms chosen were those with very developed noses.

Turning again to man, there is one particular "signal" associated with the nose which most people are aware of consciously. When someone has abused alcohol over a long period of time, the nose tends to turn red and assume a "strawberry" appearance. The misuse of alcohol is almost always linked to a very poor self-image, from which the person seeks an escape in the mindless stupor which alcohol can provide.

Generally, the alcoholic is dissatisfied with himself, and looks down on himself as being unworthy. The more he sees himself in this light, the more he actually *becomes* lower on the evolutionary scale in spiritual terms. The coarsening of the self-image due to the constant self-denigration in the thought patterns ultimately produces a literal coarsening in the surface of the nose; hence the "strawberry nose" characteristic. The redness of the nose and the surrounding cheek area is due to the engorgement of these tissues with blood, always the signal of embarassment. In this case the person is literally *embarassed to be himself*, and the nose colouration is telling the world that this is so.

There are happy (upturned) noses, pessimistic (downturned) noses, unbalanced (crooked) noses, and so on. Each of these characteristics is a reflection of the self-ness or self-picture of the nose-owners, and the reader who wishes to make a study of the matter need only ask himself what he "feels" or "senses" about the nose of a given subject in order to discern something of importance about the self-image in question.

Another symbol of great importance is the human eye. The Scriptures are filled with references to the eye and to "making the eye whole". There is a beautiful symbolism in the form of the human eye, which all men understand at the subconscious level. Indeed this subconscious comprehension contributes much to the feeling of beauty which a well-formed eye can convey.

The eye is the window of the soul, but it is much more than that: it is a perfect representation of the state of the physical body within its aetheric sheath or counterpart. In Europe many doctors realize that the iris of the eye responds in minute detail to injuries and illness affecting the various parts of the body. The science of Iridology has been developed to codify the knowledge that has been generated by the painstaking studies of the early pioneers of this subject. What is not generally realized is that, symbolically speaking, *the iris is the physical body*! Moreover, the white of the eye (the sclera) is the symbolic equivalent of the aetheric body or sheath, in which the physical is "set", and from which the physical derives all of its energy. Finally, the pupil in the center of the iris, through which one literally "looks out", is the representation of the higher self which we have described before. Any pupil shape other than perfectly round denotes an equivalent lopsidedness or over-emphasis on some aspect at the soul level.

The matter is far more complex than we have thus far explained. For example, around the iris are locations which correspond to various body organs, limbs, etc. These portions are directly related to soul-qualities in the higher self. When the pupil is "out of round" at a particular location adjacent a specific organ, limb, etc. position on the iris, it is possible for one with sufficient knowledge to say just what soul-quality is being designated and what efforts need to be made to rectify the condition first at the level of the higher self, and then at the physical.

When a person has marks or patches on the sclera of the eye, these are designations of locations of weakness or distortion in the energy patterns of the aetheric body. The positions of such marks around the iris exactly designate the locations of the problems on the aetheric sheath.

One of the most common scleric marks in the present day is that of the yellowish patches which are found often on persons who consume large quantities of meat. These people are abusing their stomachs by requiring constant secretion of hydrochloric acid in order to allow the appropriate enzymes to break down the protein molecules in the meat. The over secretion of hydrochloric gradually turns the digestive tract into an acidic environment rather than an alkaline one (as it was meant to be) and the excess acid is taken into the physical body through the intestinal wall. This eventually results in the yellow patches on the sclera, but these also designate locations in the aetheric body which have been weakened by the excessively protein-rich diet of the heavy meat eater.

The foregoing is one reason why those who eat large quantities of meat should carefully consider whether they should continue to do so. However a far more compelling reason to curtail meat-eating, from a spiritual point of view, relates to the Law of Karma which we have already dealt with in some detail.

Upon the human race lies a great Karmic debt to the animal kingdom—a branch of life which was made lower than man and which was entrusted to his care in order that man could teach the animals, through kindness and through example, something of the lessons which that soul group are attempting to assimilate. But man has assumed that all things on this planet, including the animal kingdom, are there but for his pleasure, to do with as he wishes. Man ransacks the earth's body for the mineral wealth that lies buried; he explodes devastating nuclear devices within the crust of the planet, never thinking of the pain this causes to the great Being on whose surface he resides; he devastates giant tracts of woodland for no better reason that to clear a space to walk; and—the greatest transgression of all—he massacres the superb animal life forms that were placed here to beautify his environment, so that he can fill his stomach with their carcasses.

This evil does not go unnoticed, and soon retribution for this wanton slaughter must descend upon the human race. Yet, even without a specific time of karmic payment to discharge the weight of the millennia of carnage, the debt would all be set aside. The reason relates to the way in which the eating of meat affects the physical body of man. To a great degree, this working out of the karma for eating the animals is *automatic*. There are chemical and aetheric constituents of dead animal carcasses which accumulate within the physical and aetheric bodies of the human who consumes animal flesh, and these accumulations are very harmful to man in terms of health. They speed aging and decay of tissues, they slow the brain, and they coat the arteries, veins, lymph passages and digestive tract. The result is illness, early aging, early loss of vitality, and death at an age sooner than would otherwise have been the case.

By suffering these extra illnesses and the early death, each human who has eaten animal cadavers (and thus contributed to their death) fully sets aside his part of the Karma that arose with the death of the animals consumed.

The tragedy is that these illnesses, the rapid aging and the early death need not occur! In the new age about to break like a glorious dawn upon this planet, men will recognize their responsibility to the lesser kingdoms of life, and never again will an animal have to be sacrificed for the sake of hunger, or find a grave in the stomach of a human being.

Much of the responsibility for the carnage among the animals rests with those who actively seek to promote the eating of dead flesh. These few have managed to convince most people that they must eat large quantities of animal protein in order to have a balanced diet. The false myth has been promulgated that man's body "loses" protein through daily activity, and that the loss must be replenished by eating animal flesh. Nothing could be further from the truth, for the human body is fully capable of recycling *all* of its own protein, requiring additional protein only during the youth phase of rapid growth, and in the case of accidents. Of course, few in the western world could survive if they were abruptly to stop all protein intake, for their bodies have lost the ability to recycle any protein due to the large overdoses of protein that they have been taking for years. In effect, the body (specifically the liver) becomes "lazy" and ceases to work at recycling its own protein, knowing that it will receive a large quantity of outside protein to use instead.

However, it would be found by any who cared to make the test, that over a period of 12 to 18 months, the body's ability to recycle its own protein could gradually be re-awakened, and that protein intake could eventually be cut to the equivalent of a mere 4 peanuts a day. Many could even do without this small amount, but we wish to allow for variations in metabolism, and certain congenital conditions which require a minimal protein supplement on a daily basis.

Any who care to proceed with this dietary revision, and to gain the health and vigor that it will certainly bring, should begin by dropping red meat from their diet. Only fish and fowl should be allowed for a period of two months, these being gradually replaced with dairy foods like cheese and eggs.

Periodic fasts should be undertaken for short durations, the safest fasts being those identified as juice fasts or fruit fasts. Many excellent books are available on fasting, especially those by Airola, and any wishing to alter their diets as here suggested would do well to become familiar with them.

Fasting is a highly individual matter, and the person seeking to fast without supervision should monitor himself carefully, and generally not overdo the process until some familiarity with it is achieved. We suggest a fast of no more than 3 to 4 days no oftener than once every two months as a "safe" schedule to begin with.

After the white meat has been fully replaced by dairy foods, there will come a point in time when the dairy products give a sensation of "fullness" and surfeit when eaten. This is the signal from the body that the dairy products can begin to be reduced. They can gradually be replaced with the "lighter" forms of vegetable protein, such as nuts and beans (sprouts). Those dairy products that may not give the "full" feeling can be continued, for example, milk, cottage cheese, yogurt, goats' milk cheese, and the like.

By the time the experimenter has reached the latter stage, a marked improvement in his health and vitality should have made itself felt. For those in excellent health wishing to test the idea of 100% recycling, we recommend caution, and consultation with someone who is medically trained and sympathetic to these concepts. Because of the great abuses of diet which most who read this book have gone through, we do not recommend testing the "pure recycling" concept without careful monitoring and supervison.

The explanation given above for the scleric patches in the eye is understood by some medical practitioners, and it is a sad fact that several attempts to bring this connection (and other dangers related to the eating of red meat) to the attention of the medical fraternity as a whole have been prevented by the meat packing industry, which in the United States exerts tremendous influence on the government and on those involved with health and medicine. This suppression will continue until the people themselves realize the damage they are doing to their bodies by eating the cadavers of animals. There is a saying derived from the German: "man is what he eats", and this expresses an important truth about the human metabolism. Unfortunately, many of those who recognize the validity of this saying have not seen that he who eats flesh is eating death. If one is what one eats, then surely the eating of death must bring death itself closer.

This, of course, is exactly what happens when man consumes the flesh of an animal, as we have already explained.

We have digressed from the story of the symbolic meaning of the major body features because of the importance of bringing to the reader of this book an awareness of the dangers and the Karma which arise with the killing of animals for food. In the years ahead, gradual pressures will arise to turn people away from the consumption of red meat in particular, for it is red meat that is mainly prohibited by the higher laws. These pressures will be through higher meat prices, through scarcities in many areas, through increasing evidence that eating red meat is bad for one's health, or through a combination of these. By the time the Tribulation is over, it is expected that consumption of all animal life for food will have ended.

To return now to our discussion of symbols, we wish to deal with one particular aspect of the eyes which few occultists understand. We speak of the connection between the eyes and the inner traits which are grouped under the terms *animus* and *anima* in Jungian psychology. The latter school of analysis recognizes that within each person are traits belonging to both the male principle and the female principle. Thus a woman will have, in addition to the usual traits of gentleness, love of harmony, a nurturing instinct etc, at least some of the more typically masculine characteristics like aggressiveness, an urge toward self-realization, athletic inclinations and adventuresomeness. Conversely all men will include at least some of the more feminine virtues, whether they care to admit it or not. For purposes of this discussion the Jungian term animus will be used to signify the "package" of male characteristics, and the term anima will designate the feminine ones.

In terms of the symbols under discussion, the right eye of any human tells something of the animus, while the left eye represents the anima. This holds for both males and females. Thus, the right eye for a man will represent the package of traits in the higher self that have primarily manifested in the sexual identity of the lower personality, while for a woman this is the function of the left eye.

At this juncture it would be well to explain that the soul or higher self of any human being is not differentiated in sexual terms to nearly the same degree as is found in the lower self or personality. There is usually some leaning toward one or the other at the higher level, and it is possible to refer to a predominantly male soul or a predominantly female one, but the distinctions are not as clearly drawn as they are on the earth plane.

When a soul decides to incarnate by taking on a physical body, it selects characteristics from within itself to manifest through the new personality and these it allows to influence the body as it is forming in the womb, and later the personality traits that develop at the conscious level. If the sexual identity of the new body is the same as the predominating characteristic of the higher self, then there will generally be a sense of ease and comfort in expressing through the lower self. However, where the physical body is of one sex and the higher self leans heavily toward the traits of the other sex, there can be a considerable lack of ease, or dis-ease, in the conscious mind. In many cases this leads merely to a sense of awkwardness or confusion when dealing with others at the level of sexual interchange, but occasionally, when the early home life has been such as to rob the developing personality of a balanced exposure to the male and female principles, such as would be represented by happy and loving parents, a deep dissatisfaction with one's sexual identity can develop and can lead to homosexuality, lesbianism or transvestitism.

Hence, at a more complex level, we could state that the right eye not only represents the animus or male package at the personality level, but also reflects something of the animus side of the higher self as well, since it is from this level that the personality traits primarily come. It is true that a person is influenced in personality development by the nature of the early home experience, but these influences tend to be more superficial than the traits that are "inborn", i.e. which come down from the higher self.

The same is true in regard to the left eye and its connection with the anima both at the lower and higher levels.

Now, by examining and carefully comparing the two eyes of any human being it is possible to draw conclusions about the comparative balance or imbalance between the female and the male parts of the self. Where a distinct difference is noted, whether in color, shape, strength of vision, or whatever, it is certain that some state of tension or imbalance exists between animus and anima, firstly at the personality level, and *most probably* at the higher level as well. We make this qualification since there are a few cases in which, for special purposes, a well balanced soul or higher self may choose to project a personality in which there is tension, conflict or imbalance between the male and female traits that are expressed.

This brings us to an interesting point, for it can be readily observed by any who take the trouble, that a person whose eyes are imbalanced in a marked way will confront, during his life, certain situations in which a conflict or tension between himself and someone of the opposite sex is a very strong factor. Usually this will be a repeating pattern in the life-experience.

We have pointed out this correlation as a means of introducing a critically important concept to the reader, namely that one of the major purposes of earth-life is to allow the incarnating soul to observe in physical reality a reflection of its own inner traits, so that it can *know itself*!

The ancient directive was, "Man, know thyself", and it is a command of such overriding importance that it is not possible for us to overemphasize it.

The process of coming to self-knowledge by living an incarnation in physical form is more ancient than man, for it is a constant law throughout all of Creation. The only way for most spiritual entities to understand themselves is to project into matter so that they will be surrounded by a pattern which will reflect back to them their own being.

It is as if reality in physical terms were a mirror in which the spirit could observe itself. But such a mirror only exists at the physical level. In higher planes, the process by which one's environment conforms to one's own essence is not nearly as complete as at the physical.

Let us use, as an example of this process of self-reflection, a man whose eyes are markedly unbalanced. As has been pointed out, this imbalance denotes tension and lack of harmony within that person between the animus and anima principles. Now because of sexual conditioning, it usually happens that a person will emphasize those of his inner traits which correlate with his sexual identity, and will suppress those of the opposite sexual category. This will mean, in our example, that the traits normally associated with the female sex will pass into the subconscious level of the man's mind. From there, they will exert an extremely powerful influence on him, for they will literally dictate the kind of woman he will be drawn to.

Many people believe a man is attracted to a woman who reminds him of his mother, but this is only superficially true, because the mother-model is far weaker than the man's own inner female traits. When these two influences are in harmony, i.e. when the mother's traits reflect his own female side, then the man's picture of the "perfect" woman will be very strong. When they conflict, he will be torn between different types of women and usually will end up selecting one who is closest to his own inner female "package".

Now, because the inner female package of this man is in conflict or out of balance with the male characteristics which express through his sexual identity, and because he will find himself drawn to the kind of woman that reflects his suppressed female side, it is clear that he will tend to have relationships which embody his own inner conflict, with the woman cast as his own anima and he himself playing the part of the animus. The tensions within him will then find a perfect stage on which they can be acted out, and as a result, the relationship will be marked by tension, conflict and imbalance.

Throughout these conflict-ridden relationships, it is hoped that the man will strive to reduce the tensions and that he will modify and soften those of his own (animus) characteristics which are contributing to the problems. If he succeeds in this attempt, an important reconciliation will have occurred within *him* as well, between his female and male halves.

The female in a relationship of this kind will have "chosen" the man, usually for reasons of a similar kind, namely that he embodies traits which are found in her animus. Since it takes two parties to make a conflict, troubles between any man and woman who have a relationship can be taken as evidence that *both* of them need to arrive at an inner reconciliation of the kind discussed above.

If one partner is well-balanced and the other has much inner conflict between the male and the female parts (such a match being extremely rare), then it is often possible for the balanced one to avoid the potential conflict areas by refusing to play the game of "acting out inner tensions". However, such a peace is usually bought at the price of sacrificing some important quality of the balanced partner, for example, self-expression, freedom, spontaneity, etc.

An examination of the eyes of one in whom they are unbalanced will indicate which of the two sexual halves is primarily responsible for the problems in the personal life.

Take the example of a person who has the left eye slightly more closed than the right, on a permanent basis. Firstly, a partly closed left eye *always* denotes the future or present risk of heart ailment, and it will typically be found that there is a family history of cardio-vascular problems for such a person. The left eye denotes the left side of the body (among other things, of course) and the major organ on the left is the heart. Two other portions of the anatomy are also constructed by the same energy that forms and maintains the heart, namely the oesophagus and the aorta. For this reason, a partly closed left eye can also be found in one suffering from hiatus hernia (a malfunction involving the oesophagus and stomach), weaknesses in the aortal walls, and so forth.

In terms of the animus/anima pattern, the partly closed left eye will mean that this person has trouble "seeing" the female role clearly. If the person is a woman, it will be herself that she cannot clearly perceive. Her self-picture will be distorted and will not correspond to reality. There may be the feeling that she is deceiving herself about her own self.

Obviously, a partly closed left eye in a man will also designate an inability to see the female role clearly, but for him it will mean a distorted or unclear picture of the "other person" in a man/woman relationship, rather than himself.

A final point about the symbolism of the eyes relates to the rising lines which are occasionally seen on the forehead radiating upwardly from the eyebrow, usually sloping slightly toward the temples as they rise. These lines are typically more clearcut than are the usual "crease-lines" on the forehead that become visible when one wrinkles one's brow. The upward rising lines resemble more the lines of the palm in clarity.

These lines always designate particularly serious lessons to be learned in regard to either the male role or the female role in terms of earth life. Often these lessons have to be learned through considerable suffering of a Karmic nature. Where two or more lines arise from the eye which designates the opposite sex, it is almost inevitable that that person must, at some point during the life, pass through an experience of loss relating to someone of the opposite sex, and that the loss will be a hard time for him. It is expected that a great impetus to value the other sex more highly will arise from this experience of deprivation.

Before returning to the history of the race, it is appropriate to detail one more area of symbolism which is recognized by many on the earth who study occult matters, but which is discounted by the vast majority of mankind. We refer to the hand.

The meaning of the human hand in symbolic terms is of the greatest importance for the race as a whole to grasp. In the time to come, it is expected that a course in palmistry will be part of the normal curriculum of all junior level schools, and that advanced work in the subject will be available at the university level.

Let us begin by pointing out the main symbolic significance of each of the fingers and of the thumb.

By far the most important finger is the forefinger (the pointing finger). This finger designates the broad area of faith: not merely the idea of faith in God or in some religious concept regarding the Deity, but also faith in *oneself*, faith that one can *do* certain things, faith that one will be given the *opportunity* of doing them. Faith is a great gift to the human race, made from a level of being far beyond anything that can be imagined on the earth plane. Without faith, man could have accomplished none of the great stages of his civilization, and no spiritual progress could have been made. For it is man's faith in himself, his belief in his own worth and the possibilities open to him, that literally provide the energy to keep him struggling forward against the obstacles that reality casts in his path.

When in any soul this gift of faith is not firmly rooted, then progress is slow, defeatism is a strong tendency, and pessimism clouds the pictures that the mind should be casting forward into the future to pave the way for real action when the time comes. This latter concept may seem obscure, but an important truth is being sketched: when man *visualizes* a circumstance, a situation, a goal which he wants to achieve, he literally creates a thought-form in the aether of space which draws that circumstance etc to him. Without faith that the desired situation can come about, there is little incentive to continue to picture the goal toward which he is striving, and failure is the inevitable result.

A lack of faith in this sense is indicated by a poorly formed or short forefinger. The idea of faith in God or in some higher reality is specifically designated in the nail (end) phalange of the forefinger, by the nature of the ridge pattern which is found there. The ridge patterns of the various fingers are the marks by which law-enforcement agencies keep track of criminals, but few now alive are aware of the underlying spiritual significance of these strange marks. It is true that no two fingerprints are exactly alike, and this is due to the fact that no two souls are exactly alike. In the case of the forefinger the pattern on the end or nail phalange shows the maximum point that has ever been reached by the soul (in all of its physical incarnations) in terms of a faith in the Deity or in the existence of some reality higher than the earth plane. The least degree of achievement in this area is shown by a simple "hump" pattern, in which the ridge lines do not form themselves into a clear loop or a whorl. The maximum achievement is the whorl which is formed by concentric rings. Intermediate levels are shown by the various loop configurations; the greater the achievement, the higher the loop rises up the finger.

It is essential to understand that these ridge patterns show what was achieved in past earth-experiences. It often happens that, though a soul has made great progress in the area of faith in previous lives, nonetheless in the present it has projected itself into a situation in which little or no faith in God is developed. Usually this situation arises where a soul feels that its faith in the Deity needs to be tested. Thus, when there is a whorl or a high loop on the faith finger of one who professes atheism or agnosticism, it can be taken as inevitable that the person will have to pass through one or more traumatic experiences that will constitute a trial of his faith, and which will impel him to re-examine his philosophy.

With reference to these experiences of testing for the various primary life-lessons which the fingers and thumb designate, it is possible to estimate their timing by examining closely the cross-lines that are inscribed on the phalange in question. A careful study of one's own fingers will usually reveal that one or more phalanges contain lines which lie across the direction of the fingers, often coming in from the side. Such lines must be distinguished from the crease lines at the finger joints, which have no significance to the present discussion.

It may be taken that the course of the life from beginning to end is laid out upon each phalange beginning at the inner (proximal) end and moving toward the outer (distal) end. The mid-point of the phalange represents the critical age span from 28 to 32. Thus, a cross line at the mid-point of the end or nail phalange of the forefinger will point to the likelihood of a major test of one's faith in God around age 28 to 32. The proportionality of length to years holds quite well except for the latter part of the life, where it is more difficult to judge the age at which a test will arise.

It is appropriate now to explain the major lesson areas of the other fingers, bearing in mind that the ridge pattern meanings apply in the same sense as already explained for the forefingers, and that the cross-lines of testing are also applicable. The mid-point is always in the age span 28 to 32.

The middle finger of the hand (the longest one) relates generally to the area of the self-image, which we have already touched on in relation to the nose. The end phalange (nail phalange) designates the self-image in terms of its dependence upon the male-female interchange. Let us explain this further. We have said that each human harbors within him both male and female characteristics and that it is possible to group these under the Jungian designations of animus and anima, respectively. When a person emphasizes one of these inner "packages" too strongly and suppresses the other into the subconscious then the result is, in a sense, that only "half a person" is manifesting. This occurs in many "macho" men, for example, or in women who cultivate the "clinging vine" or the "temptress" images. Such persons are, as it were, standing only on one leg. This image is a good one, for although it is possible to stand in such a manner for a limited time, the point usually comes where balance is lost. The slightest nudge is enough to destroy equilibrium and if the attempt is made to stand in this way with the eyes closed, it is found to be practically impossible.

All of these factors bear a symbolic relation to the situation we are describing. With only one foot on the ground, i.e. where only one part of the sexuality is being manifested, it takes relatively little to knock one over. People in this category usually team up with a partner who will supply the other "foot", as it were, so that some stability can be attained. However, this dependence is unhealthy, because if the partner leaves or is lost in some manner, then our one-footed person is suddenly without the extra support. If the departure of the partner is stressful or traumatic, the shock may be enough to greatly disrupt the life of the one-footed person we are discussing.

The scenario just described is typical of the situations that can arise at the ages designated by cross-lines on the nail phalange of the middle finger. Usually a crisis in the personal life comes about at the cross-line ages, as a result of which the person finds himself without the other half in terms of a partner, and must seek within himself for the other "foot" to stand on. If he can learn to manifest more of a balance of sexual characteristics, then the self-image can weather the storm and the result will be a firmer picture of self-worth and greater individuality.

It is important to realize that we are not urging men to become effeminate or women to become mannish. It is perfectly possible for a man to retain sexual masculinity while at the same time allowing creativity, tenderness and intuition to manifest. By the same token a woman need not lose her sexual femininity in return for allowing adventure, accomplishment, athletics and intellectual achievement to be a part of her life. Indeed, the truth of the matter is that the very manifestation of these "other foot" traits brings with it the freedom to *retain* the clarity, the vigor and the *distinction* of sexual roles which the Maker intended for the human race.

Turning now to the ring finger, it will be recognized by the reader as quite reasonable for this finger to designate the general area of the affections, i.e. the capacity for love in the emotional sense. The end phalange, however, is more specifically the approach which the person takes to *money*. This may seem strange at first, until it is realized that money is itself a symbol for love. It is a token of the affection which one person can give to another. Not by accident does man have the expression "for love nor money", because at the subconscious level the equivalence between the two is accepted. Money in the form of gold and silver is also intended as a token of spiritual purity, as explained in *The Nature of Reality*, but in the present discussion we are dealing at a different level of symbolism.

Consider the matter further. This is a time when few on the earth give freely of their affection to others without expecting some emotional or material return. Many marriages are a form of barter, in which the "love" is given only *in exchange* for something else, whether it be returned emotion, sexual satisfaction, material possessions, security, or whatever. Mankind has lost the capacity for loving freely, without any demand for payment. With every quantum of "love" given to another, a debit note is handed over at the same time. "I am giving you love, so you owe me ... " is the universal refrain.

Similarly, it is a time when little in the way of money is given freely from one human being to another (except within families). There are charitable donations, but many of these are made with tax-avoiding motives, and therefore do not represent true giving from the heart.

It is not surprising that both love and money are now given only in "exchange" for something, because at a deep level of symbolism they are the same.

Thus it is also not surprising that the same finger on the hand should symbolize both love and money.

Specifically, the nail phalange of the ring finger designates one's broad outlook on the matter of money. The ability to see it in perspective, to avoid over-emphasis on money, to be generous, to value human qualities ahead of wealth—these would represent the goal in terms of the money lesson, and success in learning the lesson in some earlier physical experience would be designated by a whorl pattern on the nail phalange of the ring finger.

The events or circumstances which are timed by the cross-lines on the nail phalange of the ring finger will inevitably relate to financial worries or problems. The purpose of such tests is of course to prompt a more balanced attitude toward money.

The little finger of the human hand is one which many other planetary races do not have, for it deals primarily with the question of sexual interchange between male and female. At a relatively recent time in man's history, during the mid-Atlantean era, the hand had only the three fingers which we have already dealt with. However it was known that a major task remaining before the race was that of coming to terms with its own sexuality and therefore it was decided to provide an extra finger which would signify this general lesson-area. The evidence that the little finger is a comparatively recent addition to the human form lies in the way the hand muscles control the ring and little fingers. The control is such that it is extremely difficult to fully flex or extend either of these two fingers independently of the other. To demonstrate, let the reader begin with the hand held open. First, curve the forefinger down toward the palm while keeping the other fingers extended. Next do the same with the middle finger, and then with the ring finger. Most people will be able to accomplish the exercise this far. But when it is attempted to curve the little finger down toward the palm, it will be seen that the ring finger automatically curls as well. This linkage in movement between the ring and the little finger is due to the fact that they have existed as separate digits for a much shorter time than have the other fingers.

Yet even the other fingers have not always been present on the human hand. Indeed, the hand of man when initially formed contained only the thumb as a separate articulating portion. In addition to the thumb was a large gristly mass which over the millennia became differentiated into the four fingers. The first finger to be "separated out" was the forefinger, for it was needed as a measure of the degree of faith which each human acquired, faith being the first of the great gifts which was conferred on the race. Next in order came the middle finger, the separation of this digit occurring over the period just after the Temptation, as the sense of individuality was being developed. Since individuality requires a strong self-picture and a feeling of self-worth, it is clear how the significance of the middle finger arises.

The separation of the middle finger in effect left a portion which resembled a finger but was thicker and less flexible than the other fingers. This "remainder" was eventually to become the ring and little fingers, but first it was necessary for the race to work on developing the ability to love another without having the love influenced or beclouded by sexual considerations and the self-indulgent attitudes which many humans still harbour to this day in connection with the sexual act. It has been a long hard struggle, and success is still some distance off for the race as a whole. However, when the point was reached where a minority of humans had learned to distinguish between love at the emotional level and "love" at the physical or sexual level, it was decided to signal this stage by allowing the final two fingers to be separated from each other.

Yet man is a curious creature, for when he marries he wears on his left hand a symbol of the binding together of the little and ring fingers: the wedding ring. It may be of interest to know that in the early stages of the separation between these two fingers, a person who married would wear a single ring around both of the fingers, to signify that thenceforth a single other person (the mate) would receive both his emotional and his physical (sexual) love. The wedding bands that man wears today are the direct descendants of those earlier two-finger rings.

We have stated earlier in this book that the galactic colonists at Tiahuanaco had only three fingers on their hand. In that case, however, the "missing" finger was that corresponding to the human ring finger, because the colonists were among the group of civilizations who had developed along the mental side of the triangle, and had never fostered in themselves a sufficient capacity for emotional love to warrant the development of a corresponding finger. They did however have a "little finger" equivalent, because they were in two sexes, and used a procreative process akin to that on this planet.

We come now to the thumb, which in many ways is the most significant part of the hand in terms of the great pilgrimage that man has made from his early beginnings to the present day. The thumb is equated to *energy*, pure and simple. It is by virtue of the force and drive symbolized by the human thumb that all of the major accomplishments of the race have been made. Without this energy, no progress, no evolution, no spiritual victory could have been won. It is literally the energy flowing through the thumb that has resulted in the thumb being so much stronger than the other fingers and which has given the thumb the great measure of independent movement which it has.

Energy is essential to progress. But equally essential is the need to learn to control the energies which course through the human being, not just at the physical, but at the emotional and mental levels as well. These energies, if uncontrolled, can lead to great sorrow, to the inflicting of pain on others, and to untold damage in terms of the earth environment. It is among the great lessons of the human race to arrive at last at a point where the *mind* controls the *energy*, rather than the reverse. Many men on the earth today have serious difficulties in terms of self-control, and this is due to the fact that they have not, in prior incarnations, or in the present one, put enough effort into learning to be *masters of themselves*. Nothing less will suffice for the human race. Until man realizes that servitude to his physical inclinations, his emotional binges, or his mental imaginings makes him little better than a slave, he can never exert himself to overcome his thralldom for he will not recognize it as such.

One of the primary measures of this self-control is the ability to avoid the feeling of irritation that tends to arise in the face of life's many annoyances. The nature of many humans on the earth is such as to cause exasperation and resentment on the part of others. The ability to "turn off" any such feelings of anger or irritation is shown by the nail phalange of the thumb. To be able to "turn the other cheek", as the Master has said, is the supreme accomplishment in terms of the lesson symbolized by the thumb, and woefully few men now on the earth have even become aware that the need to learn it exists, let alone mastered it.

As with the other fingers, cross-lines on the nail phalange of the thumb denote times in the life when the ability to control exasperation and irritation is tested, usually by having the person placed in a situation with on-going irritations and annoyances in it, either from other people or simply from the nature of the life pattern at that time.

The other phalanges of the fingers and thumb also denote spiritual lessons, but these are of a minor nature when compared to the primary soul-tasks denoted by the nail phalanges.

It might be of interest to know the significance of the nails themselves in terms of these lessons. The nails are, in a sense, the "armor" which the soul dons when it has learned any given one of the lessons. Perfectly formed nails (large, good color, not cracked etc) are evidence that the particular lesson has been learned at least at the level of the higher self; whereas a nail that is bent, cracked, discolored, small or in some other way abnormal signifies that work has yet to be done in the area designated.

This brings us to a further fact about the human hand, namely that the fingernails are connected by astral paths to all of the major organs of the body, and reflect quite accurately any major difficulties which have arisen or may potentially arise in those organs.

We will start with the thumb, of which the nail is connected with the lungs. The left thumbnail denotes the left lung, the right thumbnail the right lung. Any serious deficiencies or flaws in a thumbnail will show an actual or potential lung condition. At the symbolic level, the lungs correspond to energy, since they are directly responsible for obtaining the energizing prana from the aether, as well as the oxygen which is used for the oxidation of carbohydrates. Because the soul knows that the lungs have this function, any difficulty involving the lungs will act as a reminder to the higher self about the soul lesson of energy. Where a soul still has a major difficulty in controlling energy (i.e. self-control), it is common for the body to be deliberately formed with a weak respiratory system, precisely to keep the higher self reminded of the need to control the energies. It is thus perfectly in accordance with this deep symbolism that the thumbnail should be, firstly, on the thumb (which equals energy) and, secondly, connected to the lungs (which also represent energy).

The nail of the forefinger is connected astrally with the heart and spine, because it is these organs (particularly the spine) that are equated to the concept of "determination", in the sense of having a conviction or faith that such-and-such is possible. Without this faith, no action could be followed through and little spiritual progress could be attained. One might think that the heart would be better shown on the ring fingernail, but there were reasons for arranging the connections differently, primarily relating to the relatively recent differentiation of the ring finger from the little finger. Thus the nail of the forefinger shows the actual or potential health condition of the heart and spine.

The middle finger nail is related to the kidneys and the intestinal tract generally, as well as to certain portions of the neck and head. The connection with the kidneys on a symbolic level can be understood when it is realized that the kidneys themselves denote the facility of self-expression. The ability to manifest and "get out" that which is within one is clearly represented by the kidneys, which play such an important part in the elimination process. As an aside it can be pointed out that kidney problems are *always* associated with the holding in or holding back of something that should have been expressed —the "bottling up" of emotions, thoughts, talents, abilities, criticism, creativity, or whatever. When a person holds in that which urges toward expression, the damming up of this internal river is reflected in a malfunction of the kidneys.

Now, we have said that the middle finger is related to the

self-image, the feeling of self-worth, and the process of individualization. Part of the individualization process is to express that which is within, that which makes one different from all others. Without this freedom to manifest differences the differentiation process would never have begun. It is thus reasonable that the middle fingernail should denote the condition, actual or potential, of the kidneys.

The connection with the neck and head is a little more obscure, but can be explained in terms of the individualization process as well. During this process through many lives on the earth, each soul must learn to think of itself in a different way —not as merely part of a larger group, but as sufficient and worthy by itself. This revolution of conceptualization is a major step for each soul, and since concepts and thinking are mental activities, it is reasonable that the head should be denoted by the middle fingernail along with the kidneys.

Finally the connection with the intestine can be explained in terms of the symbolism of the G.I. tract itself. This symbolism is essentially that of the "path" which one charts through life. In a symbolic way, each person starts out on his path and (it is hoped) ascends higher and higher through many vicissitudes, changes, and meanderings. This can be compared to tracing the path of the G.I. tract beginning at the bottom end and rising up through the colon and small intestine, with their many folds and changes of direction. When one has met all of the various experiences of the first half of the life, it is expected that a period of "digestion" and "assimilation" will take place, during which the earlier experiences will be distilled and refined. This phase, extending from about age 28 to about age 42, is represented by the stomach. The great incidence of stomach difficulties in this age bracket is testimony to the correctness of this symbolic relation, for the occurrence of any major stomach problem (like ulcers, for example) is always meant to signify to the higher self that some important soul lesson or experience has yet to be properly assimilated, learned or understood.

From the stomach, the esophagus rises in a relatively straight path up to the mouth, which is intended to signify the hope that, after life's major lessons have been properly assimilated, soul-progress can proceed in a very straightforward manner. The esophagus thus denotes the part of the life after about age 42. Further symbolic meaning can be attached to the voice-box, the tongue and the teeth, but these represent stages of achievement along life's path which only a handful of sages have ever attained, and need not be given here in detail.

Returning to the middle fingernail it can perhaps be seen that one of the purposes of the struggles along life's path is to foster the individuality which the middle finger denotes, and that therefore a literal connection between that nail and the intestines is not out of place.

Next we may consider the nail of the ring finger, which is connected astrally with a number of bodily organs, but principally with the higher G.I. tract (whereas the middle finger denotes the lower).

The portion of the tract from the stomach upwardly is literally formed and maintained by the energies which pour through the heart chakra, which is one of seven major energy centers in the body that we will be describing subsequently. Through the heart chakra come those impulses and energies associated with love in the pure sense. Since the ring finger symbolizes the ability to manifest this form of love, it is reasonable that the upper G.I. tract should be denoted by its nail.

Finally we have the little finger, the nail of which is almost purely connected with the respective hand and arm of the body. It may seem odd that while the finger itself relates to the sexual lesson, the nail denotes the arm and hands. Yet this connection is not so strange when it is realized that the energies that fuel the sexual drives and desires of the human being are very akin to the mental energies which are associated with communication, in which the hand plays an important part. This idea requires a slight digression into the concept of the chakras, which we propose now to explain.

Within the aetheric body of man are seven beautiful spinning wheels of energy, called in the east, chakras. Chakra means wheel or vortex, and is an excellent word to describe these centres of the life-force without which no human could exist in physical form. They are essential to life at the physical plane because they are the doorways through which energy from the higher self is allowed to pass down to the lower. In the absence of this energy transfer, life would cease.

The degree of development of these spinning windows of the soul determines how much of the "real self" (the higher self) can manifest through the personality (the lower self). When the chakras are weak and undeveloped, there is a great "distance" between the higher and lower parts. Conversely a person whose chakras are strong and open will be very much in touch with his own true being and will automatically enjoy the vitality, health and spiritual richness which this condition permits.

In a sense, it can be said that the task of the human being in earth incarnation is to open up the chakras, for by so doing, he will automatically set his feet upon the path that leads to the spiritual heights. Unless, at some time in some life, the spirit begins to seek a higher way than the materialistic and selfish levels which the earth-plane foists upon all but the noblest of men, there will never occur that awakening of the God-force within the heart, without which re-union with All That Is remains impossible.

What, then, are these chakras? They are seven in number, as we have said, and are visible, to those whose psychic vision has been awakened, as coruscating, shimmering wheels of beautiful color, ever moving and dancing, singing the glorious song of life. But only in the spiritually developed person do they appear thus. Sadly, most men today upon the earth have so turned from their own higher selves that their chakras are but weak glimmers in the darkness with which they have surrounded themselves, guttering like faint candles in the wind. Is it any wonder, with man's life-windows so closed and weak, that there is so much sickness, sadness and negative feeling in the world?

In the new age soon to open upon this planet, men will find again the key to their own spirituality, and will earnestly seek to open themselves to all higher light, knowing that by that road only can they come at last to the goal of their incarnational process: to escape from the wheel of rebirth, to be done with the entrapments which physical experience sets out for the unwary, and to journey on to the astral lands where learning is play, play is joy, and joy is to exist in the smiling countenance of the Most High!

The most important of the seven chakras for humanity at its present stage is that which is associated with the heart. The heart chakra is that which primarily allows the passage of soul-energies related to the love side of the triangle. Man has universally associated the heart organ with the concept of love and tender emotion, even though ostensibly it is merely a muscle for pumping blood. This is so because there is a deep understanding in all men at the subconscious level concerning the significance of the heart. Moreover, it is universally observed that the heart is strongly affected in its rhythm by the emotion of love. The reason for this effect is simply that the love energies from the higher self which feed into the personality through the heart chakra are literally responsible for keeping that physical organ in good health and for regulating its beat. Whenever one finds heart trouble, palpitations, cardiac weakness, tachycardia, angina pectoris, heart attack or any of the other ailments which center on the heart, one can be sure that the love energy being contributed by the higher self is either reduced or disturbed in some way. Usually this will arise because at the higher self level the love energy is incomplete or unbalanced, i.e. the soul or higher self has some major task of learning yet to accomplish in terms of the love side of the triangle. In rarer instances the love is in balance at the higher level, but is allowed to manifest down in a disturbed manner in order to test the personality's ability to recognize the problem and take action to correct it.

The energy which feeds through the heart chakra moulds the heart itself during the foetal stage in the womb of the mother. When the heart is weak, malformed, subject to ailments of various kinds, there was invariably a shortfall of heart-energy during the nine months prior to birth, while the energies of the soul later to occupy the body were being tapped to form the physical vehicle. (at first breath)

All of these connections between physical conditions and higher imbalances are of great use to the soul during earth incarnation. Firstly, the deficiencies of the physical give rise to no karma on the part of some other entity, for no other being decrees that this person shall have this weakness, that one shall have some other, etc. The souls themselves create their own bodies, and it invariably happens that, where the soul is deficient or unbalanced, so in the corresponding location will the physical body be malformed or weak. The second point relates to the concept of earth-plane existence as a mirror in which man can see an outside reflection of his inside condition. This we have already dealt with in some detail. The hope, in connection with the physical weaknesses, is that the higher self will realize its own deficiencies by living an incarnation in a vehicle which has precisely the same deficiency (though at a different vibrational level).

While the soul is forming the physical body in the mother's womb, it is arranged that certain marks on the body should echo the "message" which the soul is imprinting onto the physical vehicle in terms of weaknesses in various organs. By far the most significant of these coded "echoes" occur in the human hand. It is not quite true to say that the heart energies themselves give rise to the hand markings relating to that side of the triangle, since the help of other entities who specialize in palmistry is required. Nonetheless, it is convenient to treat the matter at this point as if a process of this kind were taking place.

Thus we could say that, to be specific, it is as if the heart energies from the soul which are available to the foetus in the womb are also responsible for the strength, length and straightness of the *heart line*, which is the highest main line on the palm of the hand, and runs from the percussion (under the little finger) where it is normally thickest, to a point under either the middle or forefinger.

The "best" heart line, in terms of manifesting the love energies of the higher self through the personality, can be thought of as beginning strong and clear under the little finger, thence running across the hand with a gentle upward curve to terminate at the root of the forefinger. It should be clear, unbroken, unchained, and without sharp bends or changes of direction. It should not have the deep, flat-bottomed red pitting that always signifies the danger of heart attack and related conditions.

If the heart line terminates beneath the forefinger, called the Jupiter finger, then the love energies are usually warm, robust and largely free from restraint. But if the line ends under the middle finger—the Saturn finger—it is certain that much in the way of restraint, restriction and "damming up" has marked the individual's emotional life. Love is not able to express freely and without reserve, and the personal life invariably suffers because of this deficiency at the heart level.

We cannot continue with a full course in the marvellous field of palmistry, as this book is intended to be without drawings and photographs. However, those readers who are attracted by the possibility of increased self understanding through the study of the human hand need only approach the subject humbly and with a deep desire to learn and then to use the knowledge to help others. If this resolve is taken with the whole heart, the entities who help and guide from a higher level will see to it that a source of this information is made available.

The other chakras are of course of similar importance, since each has its function, each represents a certain kind of energy from the higher self (some are purely one side of the triangle, others are mixtures) and each directly maintains the health and function of its respective organs in the body.

There are two chakras in the head. That in the middle of the forehead is called ajna in the eastern tongue, and is what men have called "the third eye". It is indeed the organ of sight at a psychic or aetheric level, and can be raised in vibration to the point where auras and aetheric shapes can be readily seen. A few humans now on the earth have this gift as a birthright, a reward for a previous life dedicated to helping others in a spiritual sense. Many others could acquire it if they but understood the eastern techniques by which the third eye can be opened.

The ajna center or third eye corresponds to the mental quality of "seeing", as contrasted with "wisdom". One can see without necessarily understanding fully that which is seen. Many of the ancient "seers" were men who had been given the gift of ajnic sight with which the aetheric portals can be opened to reveal the past and the most probable future. But a number of these "prophets" were without the requisite wisdom to be able to interpret or understand fully the visions which their psychic sight was able to reveal.

The distinction remains true today, for wisdom cannot be 'given' in the same way that psychic sight can be given. Wisdom comes only from the higher self, and is attained through the efforts of many prior lives. Thus it is that there are souls upon the earth now who have a great wisdom where things of the spirit are concerned, but who have no special gifts such as the third eye ability, clairaudience, and so forth. These individuals are those who, by dint of sheer effort in prior incarnations, have developed their wisdom and understanding to a very high point.

The signal in the hand regarding the ajnic or brow chakra is located between the forefinger and the thumb. Lines which run parallel to the termination of the heart line under the finger of Jupiter (forefinger) are ajnic lines and show a strong potential for the third eye to be opened without too much difficulty. The other lines under Jupiter, which run generally cross-ways to the heart line termination, are the wisdom lines in terms of spiritual things. These lines have been called the Ring of Solomon, and are aptly named in view of the wisdom which Solomon had.

The wisdom chakra is that at the crown of the head, often called the Crown Chakra. It resembles a fountain of light pulsing upward in the person whose wisdom in spiritual things has been developed. Unfortunately most men on the earth today have little in the way of spiritual wisdom, and the shimmering petals of light that should be dancing and pulsing skyward are all but extinguished.

The next most significant chakra for the human race in its present condition is that at the throat: the throat chakra. This wheel of light is quite developed in many people, but in too few cases are the colors harmonious and pleasing. The energies are indeed present, but because so many have not learned to hold their tongues, because so many seem to enjoy using words to wound their brothers, the manifestation of the energy is more like angry flashes with jagged fragments of red light and a background of inharmonious color in turmoil.

The development of the throat chakra to a level of spiritual accomplishment requires above all the ability to keep silent and to refrain from saying hurtful things. There is an ancient truth in occultism, which is that until the tongue has lost its power to wound, it can never speak the truth of the spirit. The matter could not be more succinctly put, because there is a subtle law governing the earth plane, according to which the thoughts with which man surrounds himself (and words are thoughts) act like a gate or barrier, allowing through only those ideas and concepts which are of the same vibration as the barrier. Thus he who uses the tongue to hurt others exists literally in a cocoon of darkness which he himself has made, and through which no thought of spiritual merit can penetrate. Until he learns to stop up his tongue, there is almost no hope that he can awaken to the truth of higher things.

In the hand the symbol for the throat chakra is found in the little finger. Where the phalanges are all of the same length and not strongly marked with cross lines, the potential for higher development of the throat chakra is present. But a crooked, malformed or heavily scratched little finger points to one who has much yet to learn in terms of controlling what he says.

We come here to the point which initiated this discussion of chakras, namely the relationship between communication energy and sexual energy. The little finger has generally been linked with both commerce (trading) and sex in the traditional palmistry books. Our purpose here is to explain the deeper levels of this relationship in such a way that it will make sense to the reasoning mind.

Before we can proceed with this explanation, however, we must introduce one more chakra—the root chakra. This is sometimes called the Kundalini centre or Kundalini chakra. It is this vortex at the base of the spine which is directly responsible for maintaining the health and vigour of the kidneys and renal system, the spine itself, and the entire reproductive apparatus in both men and women. This chakra differs from all others, however, in that it is able to assimilate energy from the earth-plane itself, in fact directly from the body of the earth. The assimilative ability of the root chakra has not always been available to man. In various earlier epochs, different chakras had this capacity. But in the present, the root chakra's ability to take in energy from sources other than the higher self has a specific purpose related to the great spiritual pilgrimage of the human race. For the lesson of separating out the concept of emotional love from that of physical (sexual) love is one of the primary tasks now facing humanity.

Let us trace this matter of distilling out the "pure" love concept somewhat further.

In the early phase of man's adventure upon this planet, he was not capable of distinguishing his emotions from his thoughts. To him both occurred simultaneously together, and no idea of separateness existed between them. In that early time, the markings on the palm of the hand were different from the present. All men had a single line running across the palm from the beginning of what is now the heart line to the beginning of the present head line (between the thumb and forefinger). Many of the simian animal species have a similar joining together of the head and heart lines in their palms, whence the name "simian line" when it is found (rarely) on present human hands.

The simian line signifies too great an intertwining of the emotion/feeling side of the nature which the mental side—too much influence of one of them on the other. Since the emotion/feeling side corresponds to the love part of the triangle, and since love can only manifest in a pure sense if it is unalloyed by any admixture from other facets of the triangle, the first task which faced the human race in terms of the love facet was that of distinguishing the mental processes from the emotion/feeling (love) process.

Through long ages the race worked at this lesson, and gradually, as it began to be learned, the nature of the palmar lines altered: a separation occurred between what are now the heart and head lines, and (on average) this gap gradually widened.

Many people today retain on their palms certain crossing or linking lines which still connect the heart line with the head line. These represent residual "pathways" in their make-up along which one of these areas can still unduly influence the other. The presence of such linking lines always points to the necessity to strive to keep the emotions from affecting the mental processes, or vice versa. If effort is expended in this direction, the task next life will be that much easier.

The great flowering of the intellect during the early Greek civilization represented a stage at which it was considered that the first lesson had been sufficiently learned to begin working on the next phase: namely, to distinguish the pure *emotion* of love from the sexually fuelled attraction or infatuation which a majority of humans on the earth still look on as being 'true love'.

Man does not realize the powers of persuasion that lie within the physical body he has been given. The body is, in a very real sense, an entity unto itself, with its own desires, dislikes and tendencies. It even has a rudimentary thinking power and can be trained to pass signals to its spiritual 'inhabitant', as many people have discovered. We will deal later with the symbolic language of the body.

During the Greek epoch, as we have said, the primary task became that of distinguishing sexual infatuation from pure emotional love. This was accomplished largely through the writings of the great tragedians of the Greek culture, principally Euripides. The latter writer was given as a kind of special gift to the race at that time, for the purpose of arousing in man's heart center a feeling akin to the "pure" love of a parent for a child. This form of all-forgiving love is at present the closest emotional state to the brotherly love or Christ-love which all men will experience during the Aquarian Age about to dawn on the earth. The tragedies of the Greek era were deliberately designed to prick into wakefulness among their audiences the emotion of parent-child love, for it was understood by those then guiding the development of the race that the separation of the emotions from the sexual drive would have to be accomplished before the next major phase—that of raising the parent-child kind of love to a universal or Christ love level—could be undertaken.

On the palm of the hand, the tie-in between emotional love and sexual infatuation is designated by a joining together of the heart line and the Girdle of Venus. In appearance, such a line begins on the percussion under the little finger, like a normal heart line, but ends exactly between the forefinger and middle finger. Usually the end portion between the fingers is almost as heavily drawn as the beginning. The Girdle of Venus is actually in two parts in those hands whose owners have managed to separate their emotional spheres from the sexual influences: a first end slanting toward the percussion from the join between the forefinger and the middle finger, and a second end slanting toward the thumb from the join between the little and ring fingers.

The linking of the heart line with one part of the Girdle of Venus thus designates one who must still put some effort into making the distinction between pure affection and that tinged by the sexual drive. The fact that the heart line joins the part of the Girdle of Venus arising between the fingers of Jupiter and Saturn signifies that the flaw being designated exists at the level of the soul or higher self, for that end of the Girdle shows the strength of the drive for sexual union which has developed in the higher self through the experiences of many earth lives. By contrast, the other end of the Girdle of Venus, that arising between the little and ring fingers, shows the strength of the sexual drive at the purely physical level: i.e. that inherited genetically from the parents. This can be thought of as the body's own sex drive, quite apart from the proclivities of its spiritual inhabitant.

In the hand of one who has managed to separate affection from the sexual drives, and thus has a Girdle of Venus separate from the heart line, the relative contributions of these two sources of the sexual nature can be judged by comparing the two ends of the Girdle.

Let us now look again at the several stages of love-development in the human race, from the point of view of the hand symbology. Imagine that the heart-line, i.e. the love nature, is striving to free itself from entrapments with the other lines. At first it is weak, and needs the extra strength of the head line to be supported. This is the era of the simian line, when the mental and emotional spheres were combined.

After a great deal of effort, the heart line is broken free of the head line; but now it is again weak, having lost its head-line anchor. It thus seeks some replacement strengthening means, and finds the end of the Girdle of Venus. This represents the era during which the affectional impulses are being strengthened by the drives of the body, even though a time would have to come when this connection too would be broken, so that love might bloom on its own, unfettered by the demands of the other spheres represented by the anchoring lines. In this analogy, as with the life of individuals, any leaning upon another for strength and support brings with it a need to compromise the true essence of oneself. That is why the destiny of the race, just as with the destiny of the manifold lines on the human palm, is to stand free and to manifest the true inner essence as distinct from all other essences, so that in the final blossoming of all that is beautiful in each soul, this planet can be covered with a tapestry of universal love in which each strand is different from every other, but contributes its own special quality in harmony with the whole.

In the final phase of the race at the physical level, to be ushered in with the Aquarian Age, the heart line of the human hand will reflect the higher achievement of brotherly love by curving in a smooth bend from the percussion to the root of the forefinger, showing that true Christ love is founded on faith in a reality beyond the physical. A few men even now have this sign in their hands, and it can be taken that these individuals are upon the earth as examples for their brothers to emulate in terms of the affectional side of the triangle.

Returning now to the discussion of the chakras, there remain two more to be dealt with. One of these is the solar plexus center, which relates exclusively to the purely physical energies. Through this vortex pour the soul-energies of the lowest vibration, which are best suited to fuel the processes of man's physical vehicle.

It is due to the importance of the solar plexus chakra to the physical body that any blow to that area is so incapacitating, for a sudden shock there momentarily throws all the energy patterns of the body into disarray, and it requires some minutes to restore them to a proper functioning state.

Another interesting condition can also arise in relation to the solar plexus chakra. Many persons who participate in strenuous sports during their early years, but who then cease athletic activity when they reach their late 20's or early 30's, find that they develop a tendency to put on weight in the stomach area. The weight is not " soft" however, but tends to form a hard, even muscular structure in the upper abdomen. The explanation for this phenomenon is simple to grasp when it is realized that, during the early athletic period, the solar plexus chakra opens very wide to allow a great deal of physical-vibration energy through to the musculature of the body, and that when the intense physical activity ceases, this inrush of energy has no longer any place to discharge and so "accumulates" in a hard bolus of gristly flesh in the area immediately surrounding the chakra itself.

A final point concerning the solar plexus chakra should be made. One of the best ways to keep this energy vortex functioning well is to practice the exercise called "sit-ups". In this exercise, one sits with the bottom on the floor (or on a cushion for greater comfort) with the feet under the edge of a chair (or in some other manner held down against the floor). The person then lies back and, using the stomach muscles only, raises himself to a sitting position, touching his toes. This is repeated until the muscles become tired. In most people this exercise will lead to an immediate feeling of well-being in the physical sense, because of the increase in physical-level energy that it encourages through the solar plexus chakra. The exercise can be made more difficult by placing the hands behind the head, but this is not at all necessary in order to improve the chakra tone. A maximum of ten sit-ups per day is all that is required to keep the solar plexus vortex in the best possible condition, given the general health level of the body.

On the hand the general vitality, resistance and strength of the body and of the solar plexus chakra are shown by the condition of the life line, which curves around the ball of the thumb.

The last chakra to be considered is that which is usually called the spleen chakra in the West, and is located close to that organ. However, this chakra, being unused in 99% of present man, is often weak or indistinct. It is expected to become developed only during the Aquarian Age, because it corresponds to the faculty of universal or Christ-love. Consider that the heart chakra on the left side of the body denotes the "romantic" or emotional kind of love which is felt on a personal level: between men and women, between a parent and a child, and so on. Conversely, the spleen chakra on the right side relates to the universalization of love, so that it embraces all of creation, and every being which God has made. When mankind learns at last to light the flames within both of these love chakras, he will indeed have reached the very pinnacle of his endeavours in terms of manifesting, at the level of man, the Christ-love which shines like an eternal beacon from the Godhead down through all of the created worlds.

On the physical body of man, the two nipples of course correspond symbolically to these chakras. Recall that a nursing mother gives to her infant from her nipples the very breath of life, in terms of the perfect liquid for the baby's needs. At the same time the baby draws strength from the mother's own chakras which are situated very close to the nipple position. It is interesting that many nursing mothers feel more "comfortable" when nursing their newborn from the left breast, corresponding to the more developed heart chakra. It is also not by accident that when a man and a woman embrace, it usually feels more "right" to hold the partner to one's left, i.e. with the partner's head to the left of one's own. This is simply due to the fact that in all humans without exception the heart chakra is stronger and more developed than the spleen chakra. By holding the partner to the left, the two heart chakras are brought closer together than if the partner were held to the right.

Another interesting fact is that the chakras in most males rotate in one direction while those in most females rotate in the opposite direction. Thus when a male and a female embrace face to face, the juxtaposed heart chakras are turning in the same direction. This again produces a feeling of "rightness", whereas with one partner turned around so that the embrace is back-to-front, the chakras are rotating against each other. Two men embracing face to face, of course, will experience the discomfort which arises from contrary chakra movement. A back-to-front relation between men is one that gives the "rightness" feeling, which explains the preference of homosexuals for this mode of embrace.

We have now dealt in detail with the hand symbolism. There is much, much more that could be told about the marvellous energies which it is capable of directing for healing and other uses, and the way in which it has allowed the development of the mental faculty in man to proceed far more quickly than has been the case with most of the other galactic races at the level of mankind. This accelerated mind expansion has been deemed necessary by those who guide the destinies of planetary races, in order to allow man on this planet to 'catch up' to his cousins elsewhere in the cosmos. The gift was also made to compensate him for the pain of the struggle he has waged over the aeons of his history.

The hand has the ability to foster mind development in exact proportion to the number of fingers it contains. When man had only the thumb as a distinct digit, little beyond a rudimentary mental grasp of his condition was possible. The hand then had, in effect, only two 'working parts': the thumb, and the relatively stiff portion that would ultimately separate to form the four fingers. The number two corresponds to the idea of intuitive knowledge, to an understanding more at the feeling level than at the rational. In this connection it is interesting to note that 2 is associated numerologically with the same concepts that are linked to the sign Cancer and the moon in astrology, namely the intuitive, feminine, feeling, receptive and nurturing attributes. It was also a time when each person was very much a part of a larger family or clan unit, this being a notion very much within the province of Cancer, the moon and the number 2.

At a subsequent stage, when the lesson of faith was to the fore, the forefinger separated to make a total of 3 digits on the hand. This was an era of great expansion of the "self-ness" of each individual, so that there would be a sufficient source of identity at the next stage, when the self-image would be worked on. During the expansion stage, the physical body increased in size, and the great gift of the soul or higher self was made to the race. The forefinger is called the Jupiter finger, and in astrology this planet is associated with expansion, growth, abundance and faith, all of which entered importantly into the racial experience during that epoch. Jupiter is also related to travel, which was another major factor in the enrichment of man's experience at that time.

Numerologically, the number 3 is also connected with the Jupiterian concepts just described; indeed Jupiter is the closest astrological symbol to the meaning of 3 in numerology. Since these two disciplines have different purposes for man, there is some divergence between Jupiter and 3 as total concepts or Gestalts.

Finally, the number 3 at a higher symbolic level designates the triangle of God-facets which run like golden threads throughout all of Creation: those of Power, Mind, and Love. Since 3 also is the number *par excellence* which represents a higher view of reality, i.e. a more spiritual view, it is appropriate that the gift of soul or eternal status to the human race should have coincided with the splitting off of the Jupiter finger to make 3 digits in all.

When the time came to work on the task of developing the self-image, the middle finger became a distinct digit, making 4 in all. The number 4 in numerology corresponds best to the planet Uranus in astrology. Both of these are concerned with individuality, with "doing your own thing", with independence and freedom. The number 4 is also the perfect number to represent the earth-plane, and much of man's experience in terms of physical reality on this planet involves the number 4. We have touched on the meaning of this number previously, and it will suffice to point out that expressions such as "the four corners of the earth", "the four winds", and so on are merely reflections of the essential correspondence we have mentioned. Moreover, men separate and "define" themselves with respect to others by property ownership, and of course most properties are in rectangular shape, with four sides.

It should perhaps be pointed out in this connection that the era of private property has been absolutely essential to the proper development of the human race, in terms of promoting the feeling of individual self-identity. Without a patch of land to identify with throughout various lives, many souls would have been unable to establish the firm concept of "me-ness" that is essential before the next phase of the race can begin, i.e. that of the reunion of the separate, individuated essences of all souls within a compound, cooperative family, while still retaining to the fullest possible degree the delightful quirks, talents and unique characteristics of each contributing entity.

Finally, the little finger separated off to make 5 digits in all. Numerologically, the 5 designates the mental or intellectual faculty in man, and thus corresponds best to the planet Mercury in astrology. The mere fact of having five energy centers on the hand has prompted a flowering of the rational and intellectual processes to an incredible degree. Indeed, the speed with which humanity has taken up the new mental pursuits has surprised even those who guide the destinies of planetary races. It is as if the aeons of only rudimentary mental understanding have produced an overwhelming desire, at a very deep level in man, to make up for his former backwardness and to pull even with his more enlightened cousins from other parts of the cosmos.

As we have explained previously, at a higher symbolic level, the number 5 is also related to the idea of balance, moderation and stability. But this is not strange when it is considered that the development of mental strength is the only sure way to control and balance the emotional nature and to guard against its excesses. In the numerological pattern of 1 to 9 which man has been given, the number 5 occurs precisely mid-way between the two extreme numbers. It is fascinating to contemplate the depths of meaning which underlie this relationship, particularly when it is realized that the 1 and 9 are both numbers of God: the 1 represents the Creative Essence as a unity, before the division into manifestation, while the 9—being the largest number in the series—designates the entirety of the manifested worlds, i.e. God as the All in All, *after* the division into manifestation. In the Christian Scriptures the Creator calls Himself "alpha and omega, the first and the last". Perhaps the foregoing numerological discussion will allow a fuller grasp of the meaning of this statement, and the "middle" position which man—whose true number is 5—occupies. We have said 5 is man's true number, but at present the number 6 is a better one in terms of his basic vibration. In the Revelations, it is stated that the number of the beast, 666, is also the number of man. By this is meant *inter alia* that the strong physical drives arising in man's physical body, and over which he has not yet learned to exert full mental control, derive from the similarities between man and the animal kingdom at the physical level. Chief among the problems which man's body presents is the great strength of the sexual drive as it now manifests (due to the ability of the root chakra to take up extra energy from the earth).

The number 6 in its best manifestation is that of emotional love between a man and a woman. In this sense its best planetary equivalent in astrology is Venus, the goddess of love. However, far too many people today allow the emotional love to be unduly guided and influenced by sexual infatuation (i.e. by how the body alone feels with respect to the partner) and it is for this reason that the present "essence" of the number 6 is that of sex. The similarity in the sounds of these two is no accident.

The reason why the little finger designates generally the sexual sphere while its nail relates to the condition of the arm and hand is as follows: The energies which fuel the communication activities of man come through the throat center and flow to the relevant parts of the brain as well as to the hand. However, the extra communication energy which is called for at the present stage of rapid mental expansion is "borrowed" from the root or sexual chakra, which is able to draw additional energy directly from the earth and can distribute the excess to the other chakras if need be.

An interesting sidelight on this process of energy-borrowing between chakras relates to the old idea that men and women should not have sexual experience of each other before formal marriage. The reason why this prohibition was introduced among mankind relates to the tendency for the root chakra, when stimulated by sexual desire but not allowed to express it, to send the resulting overflow of energy upwardly to whichever chakra or chakras are most in need of help. In many individuals, the heart chakra is not fully functioning, and the experience of male-female attraction tends to call for more love-energy than the heart chakra is capable of admitting through from the higher self. To make up the shortfall, and simultaneously to encourage the heart chakra to open wider, the excess energies arising from the sexually stimulated root chakra are fed to the heart center. This process works quite admirably so long as sexual experience between a man and woman is delayed, and in the past those who observed the old prohibition derived great benefit from the restraint in terms of a greater love feeling for the mate at the strictly emotional level. Problems arose only when individuals allowed the old tradition to persuade them that sex itself "wasn't nice". In a great many cases, the positive benefits of the premarriage restraint were destroyed after the nuptials because one or both spouses had developed the idea that sex *per se* was something nasty or degrading.

We wish at this point to speak briefly about the question of sex, in the hope that the many misconceptions regarding this beautiful interchange of energy between souls can be set aside.

Love is many-faceted, as are all things in Creation. Love can be expressed at the mental level in words, at the emotional level by feelings and at the physical level by acts of affection and tenderness. Unless love between a man and a woman is allowed, indeed *encouraged*, to manifest at all three levels of the triangle, it will ultimately become lopsided or twisted, and will fall short of being the beautiful crown which it was meant to be for the interchange between the sexes. In terms of the physical level of love, we by no means refer only to the sex act itself. A gentle touch, a kiss on the cheek, merely hugging someone you are fond of—these are all ways in which the body, which is the instrument of all manifestation at the physical level, can express love and affection. Between a man and a woman these manifold ways of allowing love to manifest are just as important as is the supreme act of tenderness: the sexual embrace. Having said this, however, it is necessary for us to point out that the sex act itself accomplishes certain effects throughout the various bodies and levels of both partners which the lesser expressions of affection do not.

In the first place, there is the matter of balancing the excessive male and female "charges" which build up in the physical body due to the constant stimulation of the root chakra through its ability to derive additional energy directly from the earth's body. If this sexual tension is not released in a male-female embrace, it will begin to harden or calcify, so-to-speak, and will create thought-forms at the emotional or feeling level which tend to warp the outlook on life, to deteriorate one's relations with others, and so forth. For a balanced life relatively free from this kind of off-centering influence, a regular sexual release with a partner is absolutely necessary. However, it must occur with someone for whom emotional and mental affection are also experienced. If the attraction is only or mainly physical in vibration, then only the physical side of the built up tension will be released. The other facets of that triangle will remain in a state of great tension and warpage until the sexual embrace is experienced in a balanced relationship, with all three sides to its nature.

It must be understood that we are not suggesting that those not currently able to express the sexual tensions in the manner we have described must go out and look for any partner, merely in order to achieve the release. Casual sex is extremely damaging to the personality, for the very reason we have just described, namely that the only level of release is physical. Without a relationship of exclusivity and trust, which has lasted some time, the emotional side of the love tension will not *allow* itself to release because of lack of trust. Thus, imbalance is sure to result.

Nor are we advocating promiscuity, for this habit does not even allow the physical side of the tension to express itself properly. Unless the body can become familiarized with the energy patterns of the partner (through repeated sexual interchange with a single other person), it cannot adapt itself fully to the sexual embrace and many physical tensions are bound to remain even after orgasm has been achieved.

Finally we should point out that the release of sexual tension in the act of love constitutes a "giving" of each partner to the other in a very real sense. We have spent considerable time in this book explaining that each individual includes a male and a female side. However, the root chakra energies, and the tensions which they build up, tend to be strictly of the one sexual identity (i.e. that of the body). As a result, there is an emptiness in each individual regarding the root chakra energies corresponding to the opposite sex. During orgasm, there is a *literal* interchange of these energies between the man and the woman, so that the emptiness in each gets filled. This is part of the reason for the "completed" feeling which is often experienced after the sexual embrace by two who cherish each other at all three levels.

Before returning to trace the history of the race subsequent to the era of mountain-building 26,000 years ago, there is a final area of body symbolism which should be explained. This area relates to the leg. In the leg are three main bones: the tibia and fibula in the lower leg, and the femur in the upper. The knee connects the lower with the upper bones and includes a knee-cap, or patella. All of these skeletal members are of the greatest importance symbolically, as will be seen from what follows.

The human being, as we have said, is composed of a lower self or personality and a higher self or soul. These two parts are connected by energy-lines which, in a sense, pass through the chakras we have just described. When the chakras are open and strong the communication between the higher and lower is good, and vigor and general good health result. When the chakras are weak and closed, communication is poor, and lethargy, mental imbalance, and ill health tend to be produced at the personality level.

In the leg, the femur is the symbolic equivalent of the higher self. Any diseases affecting the femur show an imbalance or problem in the higher self which is, at the time of the difficulty, being struggled with through the life pattern of the physical personality. The femur is connected at the top with the pelvis in a ball-and-socket arrangement. The pelvis, being the first recipient of the creative sexual energy coming through the root chakra, symbolizes the "Creative Forces" at a level above that of the human soul or higher self. This may be thought of as the Creator-God. Difficulties at the joint between the femur and the pelvis show a lack of openness of the higher self to receiving input from still loftier levels. (Problems directly affecting the pelvis, however, tend to be related to an energy warpage in terms of the root chakra itself, and thus do not extend the "higher" symbolism any further.)

The lower leg represents the two-fold division of the lower personality into animus and anima. Generally speaking, the tibia (the shin bone), being to the fore of the leg and easily felt through the skin, represents the part that is being allowed to manifest through the personality. In a man, this is normally the animus or male "package", while in a woman it is the anima or female side.

The other lower leg bone, the fibula, is very much hidden behind the shin bone, and is very difficult to feel with the hand, except close to the knee and just above the outside of the foot. This hidden bone represents the other side of the animus/anima combination, the part usually suppressed.

Thus for a man, the hidden fibula denotes the female or anima characteristics of sensitivity, emotionalism, domestic and nurturing urges, and receptivity. For a woman this recessed bone relates to the male or animus traits of assertiveness, athletic leanings, rationality and practical creativity.

When injuries or diseases of the lower leg occur, it is possible to judge, on the basis of the bone involved, which area of the personality development is being pointed out to the individual as needing more effort. In the latter connection, it can be taken, in better than 98% of the instances, that injuries to the lower leg are directly manipulated from a higher level in order to stress to the individual some important point relating to the balance, suppression or incompleteness of the animus/anima composite within him.

Many lower leg accidents occur among children at around puberty. When these take place, it is almost invariably to remind the individual, at the subconscious and higher self levels, to correct some developing imbalance in the personality which is arising due to the peer-pressures, family pressures or rapid organic changes that are occurring at that time. Often it is due to a tendency to suppress the characteristics of the opposite sex, due to the influence of other children, in particular the patterns of behaviour that have been adopted by the peer group.

Lastly, the knee cap itself holds a particularly important place in the symbolism we are dealing with. The knee in general designates the kind of communication which is able to take place between the lower and higher selves, since it occurs between the bones which represent these facets of the individual. Any knee problems point to a difficulty being experienced in terms of allowing higher self energies to express through the lower personality. Whenever pain is felt in the knee, it symbolises the "painful" bottling up or blockage of something from the higher part which is trying to manifest, but cannot due to the attitudes or inclinations which the personality has developed. The patella (knee cap) itself is the concrete symbol of the channels or "pipes" along which the higher urges pass to the lower self. Indeed the knee cap in actuality *transmits* muscular force from the muscles above the knee to the tibia, in order to straighten the leg. When the leg is straightened, the upper leg is "in line with" the lower leg, and this relationship represents the hoped-for alignment of the higher and lower selves through the full and proper use of the channels for energy, which are represented by the patella or knee cap.

In those occasional instances where chronic conditions arise in the knee cap itself, particularly where the knee cap has to be amputated, the message is that, through disuse, the channels which connect the lower self to the higher have become permanently atrophied, damaged or closed. This is a signal of supreme importance to the individual, for unless great effort is quickly expended in seeking to re-establish contact with one's higher part, there is a serious risk that the personality itself could literally be lost, so that it would not, after death, become a part of the higher self's composite picture through assimilation. In such (rare) instances, the loss of the personality is mourned deeply by all those who from higher levels cherished it and watched over its development. We refer here to the guardian angel and the other, human helpers who have contributed to the personality's progress.

This brings us to an area which we have deliberately left until this point in the book, for to properly grasp the concepts of death, subsequent astral experiences, the still later sojourn in the Land of the Golden Light and then the return to physical incarnation in a new body, requires a good grounding in terms of the difference between the personality and the higher self.

Let us then look at the adventures which await when the door of death is traversed. Firstly, the experiences coming just at the point of death are already known to those in North America through the writings of Dr. Moody, in his book *Life After Life*. Those who are unfamiliar with Dr. Moody's investigations, relating to the experiences of those who had clinically "died" and then returned to life with accounts of what had happened to them upon separation from the physical body, should obtain his book and read it.

In capsule form, the events at death are typically these: separation of the astral body from the physical and aetheric, with the personality consciousness going with the astral form; the experience of seeing the dead physical body that had just been left; often a feeling of going through a "tunnel", which corresponds to a coming up through the heavy layers that surround the earth plane (usually the tunnel is made by those coming to greet the dying individual, in order to ease his first faltering steps into the next phase of his experience); a meeting with human or other entities who are to act as guides into the higher planes; and the "question"—invariably posed by an angel who has come to meet the individual at a mid-way point in his journey to the higher levels. The question is hard to convey in language, but it is summed up in the twin queries: "what have you learned, and whom have you helped?"

In a real sense these two concepts express the very essence of the purpose of earth incarnation: to learn and to help others. Many people go through an entire existence at the physical level hindering and harming others, and learning absolutely nothing of spiritual merit. These individuals are those who run the risk of losing all contact with their own higher selves, with the result that, after death, the personality will be so out-of-phase with the higher part that it cannot be assimilated by the higher in any way. When the assimilation is not possible, the personality falls prey to dark entities who wish to use its remaining power and 'centered-ness' to affect events on the earth in a negative way, to hinder those still living, and to drag as many souls as possible down to destruction. Finally, when the personality 'runs down' so-to-speak (which it ultimately will do because it is not receiving a supplementary input from what used to be its higher self), it will be abandoned, and will finally disintegrate and be reabsorbed into the Body of the Father (an expression denoting an undifferentiated, amorphous mass of "soul-stuff", from which new souls and soul-groups are constantly being formed). This may sound as though such a loss and disintegration doesn't really matter, because the fragmented entity is reabsorbed and then projected again anyway. However, from a higher viewpoint, the matter is seen quite differently. The disintegration of a personality after so much effort, thought and love has been expended on it from the higher-self and by the entities responsible for guiding it is felt as a major tragedy and loss. Firstly, the soul or higher self is left with less "soul-stuff" than it had before, and is thus reduced in terms of the maximum spiritual achievement it can ever hope to reach. This is so because the soul, at birth into physical incarnation, literally allows a part of itself to be cut away and to form the kernel or core of the life-essence in the newborn physical body. If the personality disintegrates after death due to an estrangement between it and the soul, then that part donated at birth is lost to the soul forever and cannot be regained.

There are a number of individuals on the earth today who will strike others as having a low level of life-force or essence. We refer to those who are weak in "being" even when healthy. These people are likely to have experienced, after some prior incarnation, just such a loss of a part of their higher selves.

If a soul loses too many fragments of itself in this manner, it becomes smaller and smaller, and eventually must be transferred to a different soul-group (for example, the animal group) who on average have less "soul-stuff" than does mankind. Continued loss of soul fragments will require other transfers to smaller groups and perhaps eventual extinction of the soul itself as a separate entity. Naturally, it too would be reabsorbed into the Body of God, but the disappearance of all the individualized experiences, talents, personal traits and spiritual potential after such long effort over so many lives is felt on higher planes as a grievous loss.

The second reason for the "helper" entities feeling the loss of a personality so keenly relates to their own potential for progress. There is a process by which the guardian of a given human being allows a part of his mind facet to incarnate along with the fragment of the higher self whose life it is to be, and if the personality is lost after death and never re-integrated with its higher self, then that donation by the angel also disappears and cannot be assimilated again by him. If an angel suffers the loss of too much of the mental faculty in this way, his own maximum potential in spiritual terms is reduced.

We have dealt in detail with this question of the loss of a personality because so many human beings on the earth today are so separated from their own higher selves that there is a serious risk that the personalities will be lost. Naturally this will automatically destroy as well a part of the minds of the angels who watch over them. It is the hope of all higher entities who care for humanity's progress that the events and pressures to arise during the great Tribulation now underway will bring about a resurgence of spiritual awareness, and a strong desire on the part of men to make up for the time they have lost over the past 2,000 years of the Age of Pisces.

To return to the question of post-death experiences, we have described the major events immediately following the separation of the astral from the physical. When the question has been asked and answered, the personality (for it is still the personality or lower self at this point) is taken to the appropriate astral level for whatever experiences may be called for to cleanse the personality of any lopsided habits of action, emotion or thought which it may have acquired during its earth life. Memory of the life just finished is in most cases clear, although the details tend to fade in the same manner as details of a dream tend to fade upon awakening. The astral personality would certainly remember and respond to individuals and places which were a part of the earth life, but there is a natural process which causes the specifics to fade from the recall, so that the events that were particularly painful will not recur constantly to the person and slow the process of cleansing that must be accomplished.

The process which causes the fading of memory is a simple one, relating to the fact that the specific recollections of earth-life events are inscribed on the physical brain during life, and are not present (or only faintly so) in the astral brain. The general "feeling" or essence of the immediate past life is available to the astral brain, because it is on the astral brain that the sum of all dream experiences in physical life is recorded. Since dreams tend to be a reworking of the various problems and conditions of physical life, as well as messages from the subconscious regarding errors in behaviour or learning which the subconscious considers the personality to be making, the result of all the dream imagery in the astral brain is an excellent Gestalt of the life just lived.

It should be emphasized that the fading of specific memory is only a temporary condition for the personality who has just died. In actual fact the subconscious storehouse, which of course remains a part of the personality, contains an exact recall of the past earth life that is more specific than even the physical brain's memory could possibly have been. In due time, the astral personality is taught how to tap the contents of the subconscious at will, and in this manner can later recall any, all or none of the past life any time this is desired.

In the early phase of astral experience between lives, however, it is best for the specific memory to fade. This may be compared to a spell of amnesia which is later cured.

In the astral realm to which the personality is drawn, he is allowed to do as much or as little as he pleases, and in whatever field may interest him. We are here talking about the "average" person in North America or Europe who has died. Generally speaking, the souls who are allowed to incarnate in these countries have earned that privilege through efforts in past lives to learn and to help others (the two purposes of physical existence). Those who are born into countries of less opportunity, or into poverty stricken conditions in war-torn lands, are those souls who have not made much progress in past lives and deserve no better than lives of limited opportunity for spiritual or physical progress. This system may appear cruel or unfair to those imbued with the notion that those who have little should get what they need free. This is a political doctrine in many countries and is just the reverse of the law applying to the spiritual opportunities that can be made available to incarnating souls. In the Christian Scriptures a statement is made to the effect that, to those who have, even more will be added, while to those who have not, even the little they appear to have will be taken away. This quote refers strictly to the spiritual level and applies to the opportunities which souls are given in earth life to make further progress of a spiritual kind.

To return then, we have been describing the typical after-death experience of relatively evolved souls. Those who are unevolved and of low vibration in spiritual terms also gravitate to the astral realms after death, but they always are attracted to the level that matches their own vibration. This law applies to all souls. Thus, a murderer who kills for the pleasure in seeing the fear and trembling of his victims is attracted to the lowest of the astral realms, which is a terrible dark wasteland, strewn with stenching carrion picked over by dreadful apparitions, where lost souls wail continually for the evil which they have done and which has so lowered their spiritual vibration. Such souls undergo terrible pain and torment, all self-inflicted by the processes which they have made into mind habits during earth-life.

But the relatively evolved individuals are attracted to one of the highest five of the seven astral planes, these five being referred to generally as the Summerland. The remaining plane is somewhere between the Summerland and the dreadful wasteland we have described, in terms of vibration. To it are attracted those who are spiritually impoverished but who have not deliberately set out to inflict pain on a large scale, to bring death to others, and the like.

In the Summerland, as we have said, the purpose of the experience is to work out and work off those earth habits which have become out of balance or lopsided in some way. Thus, if a person were to have developed an inordinate enjoyment and craving for rich food and drink while in the physical body, this same desire would remain with him in the astral. The nature of the astral substance is such that it responds instantly to any desire by forming itself into the image of the things desired. In our example, the gourmand would find himself surrounded by endless amounts of the most delectable-looking food, all awaiting his pleasure. He would begin to eat, and to eat, and to eat. After hours, days, even weeks of this activity, he would eventually realize that his whole existence is now filled only with the thing he wanted most, but that somehow, something is missing. Merely to eat and eat and never be filled seems somehow pointless, like a complete waste of time. When this thought occurs to him, he is ready to be contacted by those wishing to help him to see himself more clearly, so that these lopsided tendencies can be got rid of.

We have exaggerated this example for the purpose of illustration. Most life-habits are far more subtle than this, and take a considerable time to unwind. Consider a person who has been an accountant all his earth-life but has harbored a secret wish to be a great architect for years and years. In the Summerland he would get his chance to design and erect structures, and in the process might even build up a body of experience which would be assimilated by the higher self and later, in another earth incarnation, be put to good use. Because the repressed desire to be an architect had lasted so long, it might take several years of earth time for the soul in the Summerland to get his fill of the architectural experience and thus unwind the desire that had been built up.

After all of the longings, desires and lopsided life-habits of the past earth life have been unwound and discharged from the personality, the point is reached where the next phase can be initiated. This involves a meeting with the guardian angel and others who watch over the individual, and a re-integration with the higher self. This experience sounds dubious to many ears, for there is a latent fear that such assimilation means loss of the individual personality. Nothing could be further from the truth. To the conscious personality, the experience is just like recovering from a bout of amnesia. The personality suddenly remembers its past life in detail (and any others it cares to concentrate on), and feels as if it had finally been made complete and whole. No feeling of "absorption" or "submergence" is experienced, for indeed the event is more like an emergence, into full recall of who one really is and where one has been. It is an experience of great joy.

In this clarified and completed state the integrated individual is in a position to contribute to the discussion regarding the most suitable next phase. For many this involves reincarnation as soon as a suitable body is available. For others, it includes a brief exposure to the vibrations of certain spheres close to the earth which are associated with the planetary meanings in astrology. It is not strictly true that the soul actually visits the physical planets, although it is convenient to imagine something of the sort.

Each one of these spheres has its own characteristic which it can impart to souls who expose themselves to it. For example, in the sphere which is closest in essence to the planet Mars, the vibrations are harsh, powerful and energizing. When a soul has grown weak through laziness, or through long illnesses in physical incarnation, or again through the development of habits of reticence and an obliging nature to the point where others take too great an advantage of the individual when in earthly incarnation, a term exposed to the vibrations of the "martian" sphere would be undertaken in order to brace up the fiber of being, to toughen the individual and to give him a drive to stick up for himself and not be taken advantage of. This contribution from the Martian energy, which most souls have required from time to time, is an essential one, for it has allowed the development of the individualized human being at a faster pace than would otherwise have occurred. We have already explained the importance of the process of individuation and differentiation of each human soul from all others, prior to the re-uniting of the human family during the Aquarian Age.

The other planetary spheres have their own specific contributions to make. Thus a term exposed to the Venus emanations softens the love nature and melts the walls of insulation which many souls have wrapped around themselves as protection against the emotional pain experienced in past lives. Mercury quickens the mental processes, a procedure that is of the greatest importance to man, for without a certain strength of mind, there is no hope of ever being able to control and direct the abundance of emotional energy which the eons of human experience have unleashed. The Moon contributes an appreciation for the concepts of nurturing and protecting others, particularly children, and gives a strong feeling for the importance of a secure home environment for the developing personality. The Sun strengthens the will, and gives to those under its influence a strong desire to express that which is within. This can be a critically important addition, because it is vital to soul-growth for the individual to learn to release all that which arises within in terms of artistic, communicative and creative drives. The planets Jupiter, Saturn, Uranus, Neptune and Pluto also have their particular vibrations, and correspond to spheres which the soul can experience prior to re-birth into the physical plane. However these influences are more subtle than the five we have explained in detail, and affect more the subconscious or deeper levels of being. The language we are using here is inadequate to convey a true picture of the nature of these very complex vibrations.

Just before the birth into the earth plane, arrangements are made to have the first breath of the newborn infant take place as close as possible to a point in time which will yield an accurate astrological chart to any competent astrologer who later undertakes the computation. During the final months of the pregnancy, when as much as possible can be foreseen about the life about to be initiated, the weeks surrounding the "expected" birth-date are scoured for a suitable planetary pattern that will match the likely inborn traits, the planned karma and expected acquired tendencies of the new personality. Then, the birth events are orchestrated, so-to-speak, from a higher plane to bring about the first breath at the "best" time from an astrological point of view. Sometimes human free will intervenes to throw out the timing which the Guardian and the Helpers have planned, but these instances are rare. When they occur, the astrologer is expected to be able to 'rectify' the chart on the basis of the life-events already experienced by the time the chart is to be done.

A further point needs to be made about the question of astrological influences. In *The Nature of Reality*, it is stated that the planetary bodies have no actual or physical influence on the incarnating individual in the sense of cause-and-effect. While this is true in the area of progressions, tertiaries and the other 'theoretical' directions to the natal chart, it is not true of transits, nor of the essential influences of the planets on the future personality-influences which arise at the instant of the first breath. Let us be more specific here, for the sake of those readers whose knowledge of astrology is deeper than the average. The planets Mercury, Venus and Mars, which of course represent the Mental, Emotional and Physical (Energy) levels of the human being, are capable of literally adding to the embryonic personality certain "overlays" which may reinforce, negate, or in some other way alter the traits which the personality will develop in the lifetime about to be initiated.

Let us be even more specific, using an example. Suppose a soul about to incarnate knows that it has been far too controlled and rigid in terms of the affections in previous lives, and realizes that this tendency is a form of lopsidedness which is a hindrance to its further spiritual progress. In such a case the soul may agree to be born at a time when the planet Venus is in the sign Pisces, knowing that the 'overlay' which this placement produces is one which tends to soften up the emotions, to enhance the feeling nature, and even (in the extreme) to produce a tearful sentimentalism over things which others pass off as unimportant. Thus, the planetary placement of Venus in the watery, emotional sign of Pisces would be counted on to help modify the more normal rigidity and hardness at the soul level by producing its opposite in the personality. In so doing, the hope is that somewhere a balance will be struck, and a middle way between these extremes will be found.

Another example will allow a further insight into the matter under discussion. Suppose this time that a soul has had, over many past lives, a tendency to over-emphasize sex, to seek only self gratification in the sex act, and to lose sight of the real nature of this form of exquisite sharing between a man and a woman. In this instance, the soul may decide that the way to correct the over-emphasis is to be born under a planetary configuration which stresses the exact same tendency, but to a more marked degree. Thus, the soul may arrange to be born while the planet Mars is in the sign Scorpio, knowing beyond a shadow of a doubt that this placement will greatly increase the sex drive of the personality, and make it even harder to control the innate leaning.

The reason for choosing a reinforcement in this instance is related to the hope that, by struggling to control an urge even greater than that which is inherent in the higher self, the individual will learn the lesson so thoroughly that the natural tendencies will no longer present any problem in future incarnations. It is a little like learning to swim by jumping in a pool with a pair of boots on, two pairs of pants and several sweaters. The person may not learn how to swim, due to the obstacles he has deliberately set for himself, but if he *does* learn, he will be an extremely powerful and expert swimmer.

This latter method of correcting lopsided tendencies at the level of the higher self, in which traits are exaggerated by virtue of the planetary placements, is more risky than the first pattern we described, as it fails more often than the other way. But, for souls who have but a few of their allotted lives remaining to them, and who are desperate to overcome the tendencies which they see as sure obstacles to their goal of escaping from the wheel of physical rebirth before all their lives are used up, the drastic solution may be the only logical way. When this form of correction is chosen, the Guardian and all those who are helping from the higher planes undertake to fill the life with the kinds of events and circumstances which will strongly prod the individual into making the effort to succeed at the conscious personality level.

For instance, in our example of the over-emphasized sexuality, a life lived under a Mars in Scorpio placement at birth would contain many adverse experiences in connection with the sex life, as well as periods of enforced abstinence during which it is hoped that the personality will strive to dismantle the overwhelmingly strong predilection toward sexual expression, due to the pain that this preoccupation, if not given expression, causes.

We do not wish to deal at greater length with the astrological influences in this book. It is planned to write several additional, shorter works through this channel, which will explain the wonders of astrology and palmistry in greater detail than has been offered here.

This completes our discussion of the experiences which are met with after death of the physical body. By necessity the description has been abbreviated. It is not helpful for mankind to know too much at the conscious level about the adventures which await him beyond the threshold of death, for this could produce an unhealthy preoccupation with this alternative phase of existence at a time when the energies and attention should be directed to the problems and obstacles which physical incarnation brings.

We are now ready to return to the time of the mountain-building about 26,000 years ago. We had explained that the upheavals of that epoch brought to an end the golden age of contact with the galactic races. The cities which they had inhabited were destroyed. Tiahuanaco for example, which had been a port city, was heaved up thousands of feet by the contraction of the earth's crust, and has not been inhabited from that time to this.

However, the galactic visitors did perform a final service for their human cousins before all contact with mankind was discontinued. This service was the fulfillment of the admonition, on the Gate of the Sun, to help to foster the mental development of the fledgeling Greek civilization. The galactic race which had inhabited Tiahuanaco arranged for a number of its members to establish a small colony high up in Mount Olympus, from where they could contact the Greeks and attempt to teach them the rudiments of writing, history and language. Although the Greeks of the time of course had their own language, it was a poor medium for communication, and it was realized by the visitors that little mental awakening could be accomplished until a proper vehicle for expression could be adopted by the Greeks. The visitors therefore proceeded to devise a language based on the native tongue of the Greeks of that time, but far richer in vocabulary and in the nuances of thought and concept that could be expressed. The language which they invented for the Greeks was man's first inflected language, in which a part of the meaning of a word is derived from a particular ending (or prefix) which it carries. Latin and present-day German are inflected languages as well. By contrast, English, French and the other Romance languages are analytical languages, in which meaning is derived from the words themselves, especially the conjunctions etc., without the endings of the words having to change (beyond singular/plural and occasionally genitive).

In order to allow the Greeks to study the new language gift they had been given, and indeed to expand upon it themselves as their need for greater depth of expression grew, the visitors taught the Greeks a sophisticated form of writing, using a small number of alphabetical letters which could be used over and over in a myriad of combinations to form the different words. These letters stood for phonetic *sounds*, and were not tokens of *ideas*, as was the case later with the Egyptian form of heiroglyphics and is still found today in Chinese and Japanese writing. Thus the Greeks avoided the necessity of having to memorize a vast assortment of different pictures or ideograms as the orientals are required to do.

Moreover, the visitors left one astounding gift with the Greeks which has survived to the present day, for the particular alphabet *order* which they insisted that the Greeks learn, together with the peculiarities of the sounds of the letters, produced a series of sentences in the earlier Lemurian tongue which described the sinking of Lemuria and the other upheavals at the time of mountain-building. The cleverness of this ancient record is beyond anything that man has ever devised in terms of preserving knowledge. No stone tablet, buried in the ground for aeons, could have remained as unaltered as the alphabet of the Greeks, which was dutifully taught to generation after generation with the same sounds in the exact same order, even after the Greeks had lost what smattering they once had of the Lemurian tongue.

It remained for a twentieth century scholar, Churchward, finally to decipher the riddle of the Greek alphabet, and his results can be read today in the books he published.

The visitors remained only for a short while with the Greeks. After they left, the passage of time dulled the Greek's memory of the true nature of their teachers on the mountain. These beings became mythologized, and the old tales were mixed with pagan legends to yield finally the myths about 'Gods' living on Mount Olympus.

In the early phase of the Greek culture just after the visitors had left the earth, the written record of these events was complete. But the intervention of periodic wars caused the Greek culture to wax and wane many times, with the result that the accurate records were ultimately lost.

Many centuries of obscurity for the human race followed the final leave-taking of the galactic visitors about 25,000 years before the present. Although Atlantis was, throughout this time, a coherent culture, it too went into a phase of obscurity when little was accomplished, many of the earlier scientific techniques were lost, and nothing in the way of spiritual advance was attained. The destruction of large parts of the inhabited world at the time of mountain building had swept away most of the higher grasp of nature's ways which the Atlanteans had acquired.

The souls that were allowed to incarnate during the millennia following the Golden Age and the upheavals of 26,000 years ago were largely of lesser advancement in spiritual terms. Those who had been on the earth in the previous phase of expansion and light stood back to allow their laggard brothers a chance to benefit from the strict lessons which physical incarnation dispenses. For that is indeed how earth-life is viewed by the soul when it is between incarnations. It knows that the earth plane is the best and fastest teacher of the soul-lessons and longs for a chance to go back to the 'school' which the earth represents.

The reason for allowing those less advanced to incarnate during this period was related to the foreseen likelihood that a particularly severe upheaval would have to be brought to bear on the earth just before the final thousand-year millennium. At that time, the necessity for this upheaval, called the Tribulation in the Christian Scriptures, was not absolute, for there was still a chance that the dreadful events of such a time could be avoided. Finally, however, about 10,000 years prior to the birth of the Master from Gallilee, it was recognized that insufficient spiritual progress had been made to avoid the necessity of the Tribulation, and definite plans were laid to bring it about.

We have been speaking of these things as they were viewed from the Angel level, at which it is possible to see the future as in a state of flux. However, from the viewpoint of the powerful entities who direct the destinies of planetary races, there appears never to have been any doubt as to whether a Tribulation experience would be required. The Tribulation had indeed been planned right from man's first breathing upon this planet as one of the five pivotal racial experiences making up the Great Pentacle. Thus it is difficult to see how this time of upheaval and chaos could have really been avoided.

We have entered here an area where it is extremely difficult to describe the concepts in any earth language. We have already pointed out the paradox of three-dimensional life in *The Nature of Reality*, in describing the meaning of past and future. Those who wish to pursue the question further may wish to obtain this earlier book. Suffice it to say that, from man's point of view, it is important to retain the notion that each person has some choice regarding his own future. Thus, even though an event like the Tribulation may have been foreseen even millions of years ago, nonetheless the need for any given individual to pass through its worst phases is largely dependent upon that individual's willingness to change those of his habits of thought, emotion and deed which run contrary to the Creator's laws.

We do not propose to say anything further about the Great Tribulation now in progress on the earth, since we have already dealt with this time of awakening at considerable length in our earlier book, *The Nature of Reality*. Those who wish to acquaint themselves with the meaning and purpose of this time of testing for the human race will find ample information in that earlier work.

We have but one more major topic to deal with before closing this book, namely the transformation which will take place at the end of the one thousand golden years which will follow the Tribulation. The Transformation is literally a change of all physical substance of man, the earth, and the star-system to which the earth belongs. The change will alter physical substance into astral substance, which is a material of far higher vibration than the physical. Unfortunately, any human souls who have not, by the time of the Transformation, increased their own vibratory level to one matching that of astral substances will not wish to accompany the rest of the race on the new adventure, for it will be too painful for them to exist under the brighter light into which mankind will have walked. The choice to remain behind will be their own, and its result will ultimately be the disintegration of all souls who do not advance with the rest, and their re-absorption into the Body of God.

We had promised at an earlier point in this book to speak briefly about the language of the body, and the way it communicates with its spiritual inhabitant. In actuality, we have spent much of the space of this book discussing the *symbols* which are natural parts of the body. The reader, having read this work through to the end, will now have in his conscious mind the same symbolic 'vocabulary' which is present at the soul and subconscious levels, and which is also known to the rudimentary intelligence of the body. Thus, when the subconscious, the higher self or the body wish to communicate something to the conscious personality, it is likely that these symbolic meanings will be made use of.

For the higher self, whose basic concern is to ensure that the personality does not shrink off contact with it so that its energies are not allowed through, the leg and knee symbols are a favourite choice. For the subconscious, which contains particulars of the life-lessons to be learned during this experience by the conscious personality, the hand, face and other general body symbols are utilized. Finally, for the body, the more direct meanings tend to be used. To understand this latter statement, we must explain that the worst forms of affliction for the physical body, about which it has an interest in informing the conscious personality, are the various thought-forms that all individuals manufacture for themselves by negative thinking and negative emotions. These thought-forms tend to center on and disrupt the functioning of particular organs to which they are closest in vibration. Thus, the emotion of anger and resentment always disrupts the stomach and leads ultimately to conditions like acid stomach, ulcers, and so forth. The holding in of thoughts etc. that seek expression damages the kidneys. The suppression of the affectional urges eventually affects the heart in a negative way. The individual, by paying attention to these symbolic associations, can perceive the nature of the thought-form he is creating, and can seek to counteract it by emphasizing its opposite through specific affirmation. In this connection it is important to realize that the subconscious, which is responsible for picking up a thought-form and replaying it over and over until it becomes so strong that it affects the appropriate organ, can literally be trained to dismantle a given negative thought-form and substitute a positive one in its place. The secret of this process is to realize that the subconscious *loves a rhyme.* In this regard it resembles a little child. Give it a rhyme it can sing to itself and it is content. Hence, the way to proceed, once one has determined the likely nature of the thought-pattern which is producing the physical symptom, is to invent a *rhyming* affirmation which contradicts the negative thought, and which is such as to build a positive image.

As an example, suppose a person is married to someone who constantly criticises him and makes repeated comments of a derogatory nature so as to diminish the person's feeling of self-worth. This may produce different forms of symptom, but a common one is for a problem with the sight of the appropriate eye to show up, i.e. the right eye in a man, the left in a woman. Now, the victim of this criticism, by carefully analyzing his situation in the light of the particular symbolic problem with his eyes should see readily where the difficulty stems from. In such a case, if separation from the cause of the problem is out of the question, he may try to make up rhyming couplets which say positive things about himself. These would be repeated (silently, no doubt) several times in the morning and several at night, until the verses had sunk deeply into the subconscious. At this point an improvement of the physical symptom should start to make itself felt.

The narrative of man's history is now complete, to the extent that this book was intended to show it. We have described the great on-going pilgrimage of the soul in man, as through many lives it seeks to improve the facets of its being. The spirit in its journey passes through many seasons, each in its own time, each having its own lesson to teach.

We would now address a final message directly to the reader:

You are a child of the Living God, even as are the angels,

the planets and suns of the Cosmos, or the tiniest flower that perches upon a wind-whipped rock. For each of His creations, the All in All has an abundance of love so vast that no human conception could ever encompass it.

To you He has given a fragment of His Mind so that you could reason and think, a part of His Divine Love so that you could return to Him at least a faint reflection of the all-embracing and all-forgiving affection which He floods upon each of His creatures, and finally the right to create, from His Body, a body of your own.

In creating your body, you have followed minutely the patterns which exist at the level of your higher self. Every flaw in your physical form is a reflection of a flaw in your soul. It is the hope—it is *your* hope, whether you would recognize it or not—that the experience of a body flawed in such a symbolic way will encourage you to make the effort required to correct the flaws that are found in your higher part.

You have come to the earth plane knowing full well that it is a mirror for your own thoughts, feelings and actions. You understand at your deepest levels that what surrounds you in terms of the circumstances of your life is merely the reflected mirror image of the states of being which are found within yourself.

You have also come in order to lighten the load of Karma which your soul carries, knowing that each illness, each emotional hurt, each mental wound, is setting aside an old debt that you yourself have erected, that you literally owe to yourself.

In your progress through the vast aeons of time upon this beautiful planet, you have trod many by-ways. At times you have risen to giddy peaks of spiritual awareness and achievement. At others you have sunk into the morass of sin, and tasted all of the ungodliest experiences that the earth makes available.

But through it all, your soul has held firmly to its goal: to succeed in its quest for spiritual light, to cleanse itself of the negative habits and traits that many lifetimes have accumulated, and to be rid at last of the heavy burden of Karmic consequence which it carries, like Pilgrim in the book, as evidence that it has strayed from the perfection of the Creator's laws.

At last you stand before the gateway of final choice. You have deserved the chance to be upon the earth as the trial called Tribulation is played out. During this time of testing, your soul will have to seek within itself for the strength, the wisdom and the love that you will need if you are to face unafraid the grim reality of the Last Days.

The fact that this book has fallen into your hands has been no mere chance accident. The Guides and Helpers who love you and who always will, have gone to great pains to ensure that your conscious mind is presented with the ideas and concepts which this book embodies. Indeed, little in your life has arisen through blind happenstance. All of life upon this earth is planned as minutely as possible, in order that no possibility of helping mankind is neglected.

In the months and years ahead of you, there will come opportunities to help others, and opportunities to learn that which uplifts the spirit. Do not turn from these chances, for they will never come again in just the same way. For many of you, they may be the last such chance that you will ever be given. We are not indulging in idle threats when we say that many souls now upon this earth are literally at the *last* fork in the road that can ever be presented to them. If they make the choice which is against the Creator's laws, then they are, in every sense of the word, lost. The opportunity will never come again.

Remember always that the outcome is in *your* hands. No salvation can ever be purchased by the suffering of another. Christ's death on Calvary was to symbolize your right to try again to do what you have failed at in the past. But *you* must do it; *you* must scale the mountain of spiritual achievement by your own strength; *you* must reach out to God—for even though He holds His arms out always to you, that by itself is not enough to save you from your own evil.

Finally, remember that the universe was created for Love. The God of All that Is wished to make souls so that He could feel His Divine Love more keenly. This can only fully occur when His creatures *return* that love to Him, to the maximum level of which they are capable.

All of the souls and entities at the level from which this dictation is originating feel deeply the distress of their human brothers at this hour, as the shadows of the Great Tribulation lengthen upon the planet. We know what trials lie just ahead; we know the risks that are to be run; we know the sorrow and pain that must visit the race.

We send you our love, our thoughts, our strength. Ask to benefit from these vibrations that are being flooded into the earth, and you shall. It matters not whether you address your prayer to your angel, to Jesus, to God, or to any other entity. All creatures great and small are emanations from the One Creator. When you ask any being for help, God knows you are asking Him.

Stand firm in what you yourself believe. Hold to your own conviction of the truth above any other source, whether it be psychics, mediums, scriptures, or this very book. The truth that is *your* truth is written in the scrolls of your heart, for there too abides the Living God. Seek only to *live* that truth, to hold your own light high so that those who grope in darkness may see, and to tread the path that you believe your life has set before you.

If you remain true to yourself, it you believe in the right, and if you place your hand into the hand of God, then no evil, no lasting sorrow, and no permanent pain will ever befall you.

May the peace and blessing of all the higher beings who care for humanity's struggle be with you forevermore.

OM MANI PADME HUM

INDEX

Adam, Eve, 12, 16, 23
Aether, 1, 26, 28, 35, 42, 50
Aetheric body, 61, 82
Aging, 20, 24, 42
Airola, Paavo, 43
Ajna chakra, 65
Alcohol, abuse, 39
Angel, 82, 84, 87
Angels, fallen, 25
Animals, 20, 29
Animus, anima, 44
Aquarian age, 2, 42, 62, 69, 88, 96
Astral body, 82
Astral lands/plane, 17, 62, 84
Astral life, 84
Astral, lower, 86
Astral paths, 58
Astral summerland, 86
Astrology, 89
Atlantis, 6, 28, 30, 33, 55
Atomic, 6

Bible, 1, 11
Body, creation, 25

Chakras, 60, 71
Crown chakra, 66
Christ-love, 72
Churchward, 93
Cosmic law, 2
Creation, 16
Creatures, mountainous, 6

Dark entities, 83
Death, 19, 23, 82

Destruction, 33
Draco, 31
Dreams, 85
Drowning, 27

Earth, 27
Earthquakes, 8
Emotional, 12, 14, 20, 25, 27
Energy, man's, 34, 56
Eye, 40, 44

Faith, 50
Fasting, 34, 43
Female, male characteristics, 47
Fingernails, 57
Fingers, 55
Five (5), 10
Flood, 27
Forehead, lines, 49
Food, 41
Four (4), 10

Girdle of Venus, 69
God, Trinity, 11
Greek epoch, 68, 92

Hand, 50
Health, 97
Health, sit ups, 71
Heart ailment, 48
Heart chakra, 60
Heart line, 64
Higher-self, 36
Hindus, 3
Hermaphrodite, division, 15

Homosexuality, 46
Hypnotism, 20

Illusion, 2
Incarnation, 23, 45, 82, 88, 94
Individuality, 21
Inert gasses, 24
Intestinal tract, 59
Iridology, 40

Jesus Christ, 91, 22
Jewish, 37
Jung, 44

Karma, 1, 13, 23, 30, 41, 44, 49
Karma, sharing, 6, 8, 9
Kidneys, 59
Knee, 81
'Know thyself', 47
Kundalini chakra, 67

Language, 92
Leg, 79
Lemuria, 30, 34, 93
Lessons on life, 52, 91
"Life After Life", Book, 82
Life force, 83
Love, 13, 53, 62, 67, 76, 77
Lower-self, 36
Lucifer, 17, 23
Lung capacity, 35

Man, know thyself, 47
Male, female characteristics 47
Meat, 40
Money, 53
Moody, Dr., 82

Nails, finger, 58

Natural selection, 34
Neanderthal man, 30
New age, 2, 42, 62, 69, 88, 96
Noah, 29
Nose, 38
Numerology, 73

Palmistry, 50, 73
Past lives, 85
Pentacle, great, 10, 95
Personality, loss of, 82
Piscean age, 84
Planetary Spheres, 88
Prana, 55
Protein, 42
Pyramid, Gizeh, 10

Reincarnation, 23, 45, 82, 88, 94
Re-integration, 87
Root chakra, 67
Rhyme, 97

Sea, 14
Selfishness, 21, 30
Self image, 38
Sexual balance, 52, 78
Sexual drive, 69
Sexual identity, 45
Sexual union, 18
Solar plexus chakra, 71
Soul, 19, 40
Soul reintegration, 87
Spleen chakra, 72
Star of David, 37
Stomach 60
Subconscious, 85
Summerland, 86

Throat chakra,
Temple, 26
Temptation, 11, 15, 20, 55
Third Eye, 65
Thought form, 50
Throat chakra, 66
Tiahuanaco, 30
Tongue, 66
Transformation, earth, 95
Transvestitism, 46
Transgression, 18
Tribulation, 10, 14, 24, 27, 33,
　　44, 84, 95
Truth, 1

Uripedes, 68

Visitors, galactic, 33, 56, 92

Workers, the, 29

Lightline
A CHANNEL FOR ESOTERIC TRUTH AND INFORMATION

A bi-monthly newsletter allowing subscribers access to the Hilarion channel. General questions sent in are answered in this publication.

For more information write

Lightline
    195 Randolph Rd.
    Toronto, Ontario
    Canada, M4G 3S6